The Devil
Did Not
Make Me Do It

The Devil Did Not Make Me Do It

Paul M. Miller

Introduction by
Basil Jackson, MD

HERALD PRESS
Scottdale, Pennsylvania
Kitchener, Ontario

THE DEVIL DID NOT MAKE ME DO IT
Copyright © 1977 by Herald Press, Scottdale, Pa. 15683
    Published simultaneously in Canada by Herald Press,
    Kitchener, Ont. N2G 4M5
Library of Congress Catalog Card Number: 76-57348
International Standard Card Number: 0-8361-1814-6
Printed in the United States of America
Design: Alice B. Shetler

10 9 8 7 6 5 4 3 2 1

DEDICATED to my many Christian friends
in six countries of Africa,
who have helped me see that fearing evil spirits
is reverting to animism, and
have helped me claim Christ's finished victory
over Satan and his imps.

Contents

INTRODUCTION

In January 1975 I was privileged to preside over a conference on demonology at Notre Dame University under the auspices of the Christian Medical Society. Although grateful for all the exciting experiences of that week, I was particularly happy to make the acquaintance of Paul M. Miller, the author of this book. In my judgment he is eminently qualified as an authority on the subject. His insights are pointed, precise, and practical.

In his personal ministry, Miller has demonstrated compassion and competence both as a pastor and as a counselor. He is an astute student of human nature as well as of the deep things of God. Trained in a theology which is committed to the deity of Jesus Christ and the inspiration of the Word of God, he leaves no doubt where he stands on fundamental issues. This in itself causes him to speak as a man to whom attention must be given. When he lovingly takes issue with the current popular view of demonology in evangelical circles, he speaks with more than usual authority. His base is not pigeonholed or culture bound to one type of life experience. He has spent a significant part of his life in Africa where demons are said to flourish in exceptionally large numbers and yet he says what he says.

The issue to which the author speaks is obviously one of significant contemporary concern. The surge of interest in the occult in the United States and Canada in recent years has been phenomenal. This increase is not only "in the world," as might be expected, but also very much within "the household of faith."

We may well wonder whether the recent fascination with occultic activities and mysteries represents an actual increase in demonic activity. If the answer is yes, we need not be surprised. The Bible indicates that such an increase occurred before the Flood and again during the time of Christ's earthly ministry. We are clearly warned to expect an unprecedented increase in demonic activities in the last days similar to what occurred in the time of Noah. These perilous times may well be at hand.

While accepting the biblical testimony on this subject, Miller wisely points out that specificity and accuracy in diagnosis remain the prerequisites for any form of therapeutic approach. The *Post Hoc, Ergo Propter Hoc* (after this, therefore because of this) notion remains the most common fallacy in the thinking of those who practice a deliverance ministry. The sequence too often is as follows: No adequate or accurate diagnosis is made; the healer engages in some rite or ritual; the patient appears to improve; therefore, the initial diagnosis of "demon possession" must have been correct. This is faulty reasoning.

The author encourages us to be slow to make assumptions in areas where we have so little knowledge. He encourages us to explore thoroughly all natural possibilities, whether of a physical or psychological nature, before jumping on a supernatural-cause bandwagon. This, in my opinion, is sound advice.

Miller shows us in straightforward, simple language the way out of this confusion. He calls for a rediscovery of a Christ-centered, Bible-based victory over sin and evil and over the "Devil Made Me Do It" disease of personal irresponsibility. He emphasizes the relative weakness of the devil, the relative strength of the Christian, and the absolute power of our God. He points out the danger of meddling in the occult. He accepts the New Testament record on demonization. Yet he demonstrates that the diagnosis of possession in our day is unfortunately often a measure of the ignorance of the one who makes the diagnosis.

Paul Miller wisely stresses in this book that the secret of victory lies only in Christ, in prayer, and in the community life of the believers who are the body of Christ. The church will do well to give close attention to this message.

Dr. Basil Jackson
Jackson Psychiatric Center
Milwaukee, Wisconsin

Author's Preface

Why did I write this book? I have struggled deeply with my own feelings because the church I love so much is ambivalent and divided about the right attitude toward demonism. My motive in writing this book is to help the church find her way out of the confusion.

I can understand why people outside of Christ and His Spirit may be vulnerable to demonism just now. The level of fear is high, and the trust in monotheism (one all-powerful God) is low. The level of guilt is great, and who to blame it all on is not clear. Many newly affluent persons are searching for meaning in their lives. Some who have experienced the best therapy which psychiatry has to offer still find spiritual hungers unmet.

Naive reliance upon scientism to solve all ills has not satisfied the human spirit. An overemphasis on intellectualism and reason has given way to a new awareness of the nonrational and irrational. A large American university has awarded a doctor's degree to a person who devoted ten years to learning the secrets of an aged American Indian medicine man.

I know that drugs have expanded consciousness. Hypnosis and parapsychology have produced startling effects. Eastern religions are having their impact. There is a new openness to the transcendent. Astrology is winning believers. Death is being studied intensely. New experiments are producing startling results in communicating with animals and plants. Seances are thriving. The attempts to manipulate the world of the supernatural are increasing on every side. We now have a generation of persons who have been reared on the near-magic of television, with its guilt-producing reporting of wars and sensationalism on every side. Exorcism fits well into such a world.

But must God's people revert to animism just because the non-Christian world does so? I know we are supposed to be entering the age of Aquarius when persons get their "word from the stars" (astra-logos). Well educated people are buying astrology horoscopes for themselves and even for their dogs and cats. Some major corporations retain an astrologer to give counsel. Some high government officials seek guidance from the positions of the planets. Many common people have the signs of the Zodiac stamped on their kitchen and bedroom furniture and on their personal effects. Youth are giving to astrology the reverent attention which they earlier devoted to psychology courses.

I believe that God in His sovereignty is calling our generation (newly aware of the spiritual realm around them) to hear His Holy Spirit and to join in the new peoplehood His Son is ever creating. It is to aid in this new movement of God in our time that I write this book.

I began my study into the pros and cons of exorcism because a devout Roman Catholic priest asked me to help him think through whether he should practice exorcisms (naming a suffering person's demon and casting the demon out by a churchly ritual designed for that purpose).

I read about fifteen books related to demonism, and finally presented a one-hour lecture to the Theological Integration Seminar in which the 53-year-old priest was a student. Then, because of the excitement generated by *The Exorcist* movie, the ministers of Elkhart, Indiana, asked me to brief them on the problem. I dug through another ten or so books and spoke to them. Following this, they asked me to address a mass meeting in the high school auditorium of Elkhart. I worked through another spread of literature for that occasion.

As *The Exorcist* film seared its way across the country, the invitations continued to come for me to speak to congregations, colleges, and ministers' groups. I have continued to study the pertinent biblical material. I have done word studies of crucial terms. I have given lectures and received questions and feedback from more than 40 audiences involving approximately 7,000 persons across the United States and Canada. I have read nearly 200 books and booklets on the subject (see the bibliography at the back of this book). I have received the warmest commendation and encouragement and the bitterest of accusation and attack from equally devout Christians.

For more than twenty years I have lectured throughout the church on issues related to evangelism, worship, missions, pastoral care, marriage enrichment, and on exposition of books of the Bible, but I have never encountered such a divided response on any other subject. I am encouraged by the fact that the teaching in this book is being widely accepted except for a small, but vocal, minority.

My best experiences have been the five occasions in which I had time to give five one-hour lectures on the subject, with an interdisciplinary panel providing feedback and raising further questions. I have always had strong support from both the Bible scholars and the psychiatrists in my audiences. Medical doctors tend to be friendly but hesitant to speak. Ministers have been friendly and challenging. College student responses have been serious and probing.

In the chapters which follow, I develop the theme introduced in Genesis 3 the first time the devil is mentioned in the Bible. It was a cop out for Eve to say, "The devil made me do it," just as it was a cop out for Adam to say, "The woman made me do it." (See Genesis 3:12, 13.)

The underlying assumption of this book is that God wants persons to take responsibility for their own lives and that He offers a way of victory over the powers of evil. Along the way, I pause to show why exorcism is less than the scriptural ideal for helping one another.

This book is the hardest writing task I have ever attempted. The range of relevant material is vast and the attempt to arrange and simplify it daunted me.

My wife kept encouraging me to go on, during the dozens of times I felt like quitting work on the manuscript. My colleague, Millard Lind, professor of Old Testament at Associated Mennonite Biblical Seminaries where I teach, kept urging me on and giving valued feedback on my ideas. Countless persons who heard my lectures urged me to put these ideas into writing.

The total feedback given to my lectures has been a powerful molder of the ideas in this book. At a Roman Catholic College in Michigan the response added up to, "Don't insist that everything mysterious about the human mind and human emotions is either divine or demonic. Allow a third category—that which is human. Admit that precognition, clairvoyance, levitation, hypnotism, and the like may well be demonstrations of the grandeur of man as man, so fearfully and wonderfully made. These great powers of the mind perhaps only become divine or demonic as they align themselves with good or evil."

The comments from therapists and staff of a mental hospital in Ontario seemed to say, "Stay by the wisdom of the Israelites and Jews as they followed their God. They have more to teach us than almost any other source about how to deal with the demonic."

The response from the students and faculty at a college in Kansas could be summarized as, "Stay by the certainties, drawn from holy history, of God's ways in helping His people to cope with the demonic. The stories from Satan-followers, witchcraft ceremonies, voodoo worshipers, seances, and exorcisms are titillating and sensational, but prove nothing."

At a university in Canada, where a vehement exorcist was in the response group, the group's total response said to me, "Stay by your emphasis upon monotheism, and show Christ's movement away from exorcism."

A minister's conference in Virginia, by their questions and comments conveyed to me the advice, "Beware that you don't leave the impression that 'it's all in your mind,' or that the devil is only the projection of mankind's dark side. All evangelicals insist that Satan is a person and is very powerful."

A congregation in Arizona could be summarized as, "We like the way you stress our victory in Christ, and give attention to Satan only obliquely. We can face Satan unafraid if our faith in Jesus is clear and strong."

So, many thanks to the many who helped me so much. I take the responsibility for the ideas that are offered in the book.

Before we proceed to chapter 1, some definitions and references to the literature in the field may be appropriate.

My dictionary defines exorcism as "verbal formulae used in exorcising," and exorcising as "the driving away of an evil spirit by adjuration" and "invoking the name and power of a higher spirit to free a person from a lesser spirit."

All religions have their rituals, their charms, their incantations, and their holy men who can invoke a still higher spirit to free a person from possession by a lesser one.

The Roman Catholic rite is a service of prayers.[1] A prayer to St. Michael is followed by invoking the name of Jesus, commanding the demons "whoever you may be" to depart, and a series of adjurings to the demons to submit! The service concludes with responsive prayers and the sprinkling of holy water.

The clergy manual of The International Order of St. Luke, The Physician, includes "A Form for Divine Exorcism," also referred to as "A Ministry of Deliverance."[2] It describes "obsession" as controlling thoughts, and "possession" as complete dominance by a discarnate spirit.

The officiant is encouraged to conduct the ritual in the sanctuary, before the cross, while wearing an ecclesiastical robe. Two intercessors, one on either side, are instructed to help with responses.

The service consists of a prayer for divine protection, followed by one for the gift of discernment. A questioning of "the subject" follows regarding his readiness to forgive others, to seek forgiveness himself, and to name any specific unconfessed sins.

If the subject is able to do so, he is led through an official renouncing of Satan. The officiant then asks the evil spirit to tell its name, and commands it to depart, in the name of Jesus Christ.

If the evil spirit is especially possessing, the officiant may make the sign of the cross and speak with firm authority: "Spirit _____(name)_____, I am anointed by the Holy Spirit to cast you from __(name of subject)__ . In the name of Jesus of Nazareth I cast you out. Now go!"

The above is repeated until the spirit departs, which is usually indicated by the subject's coughing, spitting, vomiting, convulsing, screaming, or cursing.

The officiant then prays that the evil spirit may be bound forever, and that the subject may be newly filled with God's Holy Spirit.

As a test, the questions asked earlier may be asked again, to be sure the person's answers are different now.

A variety of Protestant exorcists and "ministers of deliverance" each have their own rituals. Kurt Koch,

Derik Prince, Don Bashan, Robert Peterson, Hobert
Freeman, and Nicky Cruz are representatives of a host
of others. In many of them an important part of the
ritual is the naming of the demon (with the caution not
to converse with the demon any further), and the forbid-
ding of the demon to return.

A survey of some representatives of varying traditions
reveals that the subject of demons and exorcism is
treated very lightly or not at all. The words are not in the
index of such diverse volumes as *The Mennonite Ency-
clopedia*, Elton Trueblood's *Philosophy of Religion*, John
Hutchinson's *Faith, Reason, and Existence*, Carl F.
Henry's *Christian Personal Ethics*, Edward Carnell's *A
Philosophy of the Christian Religion*, Charles Finney's
Systematic Theology, H. Orton Wiley's *Christian
Theology*, John C. Wenger's *Introduction to Theology*,
David Robert's *Existentialism and Religious Belief*,
Archibald Hunter's *Introducing New Testament The-
ology*, or Thomas Oden's analysis of the ethics of Ru-
dolph Bultmann, *Radical Obedience*.

Most biblical scholars agree with Karl Barth that the
devil and the demons deserve only a quick sidewise
glance. After devoting 152 pages to a treatment of
angels, Barth devotes a mere ten to demons. Eric Rust in
a biblical *Interpretation of Salvation History* treats the
demonic, but not from the viewpoint of personal discarnate entities which can move in and out of a person.
Even a dispensationalist theologian like Lewis Sperry
Chafer in his eight-volume *Systematic Theology* includes
no mention of exorcism in his index.

It is interesting to observe that Martin Luther, although sharing intensely in the medieval view of

demons, presented the central processes of the Christian life without much reference to evil spirits. Reinhold Seeburg reports that "large sections of his [Luther's] sermons may be searched in vain for any reference to the devil"[3]

The sober and restrained treatment which biblical scholars give to the study of demons should urge extreme caution in accepting the sudden certainties of some recent writers.

Paul M. Miller
Goshen, Indiana

Part I

*The Devil Did Not
Make Me Do It*

1
God Controls My Life

I am a monotheist. I believe in only one God, and that He has the whole wide world in His hands. He alone is King over all the earth. There is none other beside Him.

No one else is near enough in power and knowledge to be an evenly matched rival for Him. He is running a one-party system, and there is no chance that He might be voted out of power at the next election.

He not only created the worlds, but sustains them by His power. He created every living thing, in heaven, on earth, and under the earth.

He is now, always has been, and forever will be King of kings, Lord of lords, sole Sovereign of the universe, and the One to whom every human king, every rebellious spirit, and every ordinary person must give account and must eventually bow.

He is so exalted and majestic that the heaven of heavens cannot contain Him, and yet so immanent that He is nearer than our hands and feet. The heavenly Father feeds the birds of the air, numbers the hairs of our heads, and is active by His loving Spirit in all of nature and in every living thing.

Polytheists (those who believe in many gods) never quite know which god is really in control. Their gods have their own petty rivalries and must be appeased. The priests of various religions try to manipulate the supernatural, the fickle gods and their affairs, and to free persons from the evil designs of the bad gods or demons. The witch doctor manipulates the demon of conception so the desired child is conceived in the womb. The exorcist casts out the demon of stomachache and of one disease or another.

To the polytheist or animist, since the spiritual world is so chaotic, and at times even vengeful, a demon lurks behind every apparently natural event. A demon causes every toothache. A demon sends the hail, the frogs, the lice, the storm. A demon causes a snake to bite you.

The polytheist or animist (as well as some modern deliverance ministers or exorcists) are likely to see a demon behind barrenness, asthma, allergies, blindness, deafness, epilepsy, arthritis, weakness, anemia, cancer, typhoid, gland trouble, heart failure, eczema, cerebral palsy, diabetes, or rheumatism.[1]

Since my personally known, Fatherlike God is in control, and all the world is His, I do not fear a demon lurking behind every stone or bush. I do not say, "The devil made me do it." I am much more likely to see guardian angels everywhere. If God creates and sends discarnate spirits they will be angels—messengers for good ready to help, to warn, to direct, and to inspire.

This does not at all deny that some of God's sons have gone astray, some of His angels have fallen, some of His agents have mutinied, and that there is a rebellious world of evil and magic.

Because God called His people out of Egypt by a victorious showdown with all of the magicians and exorcists of Pharaoh, His people learned to trust God alone, and to need no exorcists to manipulate the demons for them. Since God's law directed their lifestyle, economics, ecology, insurance devices, institutions, and relationships, they felt no need to exorcise demons.

Israel could readily believe that their all-good and completely sovereign God had commanded an angel to interpose a cloud between them and their enemies, the Egyptians. Although other Near Eastern religions had stories somewhat similar, Israel always modified them to fit their own monotheism.

Instead of seeing demons behind every tree, they told of good angels at springs of waters (Genesis 16:7), beside oaks (Genesis 18:1,2), and near blazing thornbushes (Exodus 3:2).

Not only did angels feed on celestial food called manna, but they helped God's people to get it too.

Not only did angels have access to heaven's joys already, being able to move up and down ladders from earth to heaven, but they helped bring believing Israelites into that same joyous experience, even through dreams.

Not only did angels gather as a celestial choir singing of God's glory and power, but as a phantom host they lingered near believers during times of testing, ready and eager to share their lives of praise and assurance of God's victory. God's people can live with the awed feeling that the very mountains around them are filled with the protecting chariots of the Almighty. They pray for one another, when testing becomes severe, "Open the young man's eyes that he may see God's encircling power."

Polytheists may live in fear of river demons and turn to their witch doctors or exorcists for help. But the believer in monotheism, whose one God is in control, finds the river spirit actually an angel wrestling with him for his own good, and ready to touch him in life-changing renewal.

Polytheists may fear the demon of barrenness, which prevented having children. But godly Manoah and his wife discovered it was God's angel who promised them a child and then went up with the smoke (Judges 13:20).

Polytheists feared the demons of sunstroke and the powers of the air, but devout monotheists believed that guardian and good angels were so numerous that they created the glowing skies, the Milky Way among the stars, as they escorted the sainted dead into paradise above.

A few devil alibis appear in the Bible. Eve's "The devil made me do it" is just as much an evasion of her own responsibility as was Adam's lame excuse, "The woman whom thou gavest to be with me, she gave me fruit of the tree, and I ate" (Genesis 3:12).

But thankfully we do not read in the Scriptures that the devil made Potiphar's wife conspire against Joseph, that the devil caused Dan to turn against Joseph, that the devil caused corruption among the sons of Job, that the devil killed the first born of Egypt, and the like.[2]

In a world where there is only one God, and He is the absolute, totally good, and just Sovereign, His people do not readily fear the "elemental spirits of the universe," whatever these powers be which are not understood and are most bothersome at the time.

One of the hymns included in the Dead Sea Scrolls glories in the fact that the good God of creation turned the feared demons of the seasons, of death, and of healing into angels. When a people's God is too small, then their demons become too large and fearsome. When God becomes again their acknowledged omnipotent Sovereign, their entire world of spiritual reality changes.[3]

I protest against most of the scores of books, booklets, and tracts which evangelicals are producing today about the devil. They are too filled with pessimism. They paint the devil too strong, as though he were really a second god running our universe. I feel sometimes that calling the devil "his majesty" and stressing endlessly his kingdom, his imps, and his demons in Christians is a worse "God is dead" movement than the one taught by some theologians.

Unwittingly and unintentionally, those who are painting the devil too large and powerful may be as great a detriment to wholesome Christian living as are the humanists, liberals, or existentialists who are painting God too small. What the Christian church needs is a renewal of her faith in God's sovereignty so that Christians really believe God is in control, and that even during life's trials the devil has no freedom apart from His divine will.

I believe that God is One, absolutely omnipotent, sovereign, and without threatening rival on the throne of the universe. He is my God, as real as a Father because of a new-birth relationship I have with Him. My own private world, my personal experience of spiritual reality (like the biblical record itself), should have twice as many angel-type visitations as it has dark expressions of the devil or his little demons.

The Father's world must be more filled with angels than with demons because "he who is in you is greater than he who is in the world" (1 John 4:4) is a reality to claim and to live by. It must dominate our lifestyle, emotions, fantasies, dreams, aspirations, memories, consciousness, and will.

I seek to stand solidly in continuity with God's people who felt themselves surrounded by angels, penetrated by God's messages through dreams, led by His providence, delivered by His power, molded into a people by common obedience to His holy will, surprised by His unmerited favor, and linked into His consummating purposes for His world.

The devil did not make me do it—because my God is in control.

For Studies of Monotheism and God's Sovereignty:
Stewart, James. *Thine Is the Kingdom* (New York: Scribners).
Kelsey, Morton. *Dreams, The Dark Speech of the Spirit* (New York: Doubleday, 1974).

For Studies on Satan, the Devil, and Demons:
Breeze, Dave. *His Infernal Majesty* (Chicago: Moody Press, 1974).
Complete Edition of the Sixth and Seventh Books of Moses (Cleveland: Arthur Westbrook Co.).
Koch, Kurt E. *Between Christ and Satan* (West

Germany: Evangelical Publishers, 1968).

McCall, T. S., and Zola Levitt. *Satan in the Sanctuary* (Chicago: Moody Press, 1973).

Oesterreich, T. K. *Possession, Demonical and Other* (New York: University Books, 1968).

Thielicke, Helmut. *Between God and Satan* (Grand Rapids: Eerdman's, 1959).

Warnke, Mike. *The Satan Seller* (Plainfield, N.J.: Logos, 1972).

Wright, G. Ernest. *The God Who Acts* (Naperville, Ill.: Allenson, 1952).

2
God Limits What
the Devil Can Do To Me

I accept the view of the devil that he is a prodigal son of God, as Job 1:6 pictures him. But, among the obedient sons, the Scriptures add, "Satan also came." He is last, he is least, and he is strictly limited by Almighty God. He is a "naughty boy" off in a far country. He cannot manipulate what Almighty God desires to do for me.

I see the devil also not only as a pathetic prodigal, but as pitifully defiant. "Job will curse thee to thy face," Satan told God. He had been "walking his beat," going to and fro in the world, but instead of functioning as a guardian angel, he began scheming Job's fall. And he schemes mine.

The prodigal son becomes the prosecuting attorney in Zechariah 3:1, jumping up in the heavenly court as the accuser of the brethren. The Prophet Zechariah seems to suggest that Satan is about on the same level as Joshua the high priest in power and influence. Other passages accord more power to him.

Far from being a potential rival for the Sovereign and Omnipotent God, Satan is merely one rebel among the ten thousand times ten thousand and heavenly beings fully loyal to God and aligned to do His will (Daniel 7:10). I feel that God's power in relation to Satan's is on the order of a million to one. However, as I smell the stench of human sin on every side, I'm momentarily tempted to feel that mankind has chosen to leave the Father's house to join the rebel son in his far-country pigpen of misery.

But I exult with the psalmist in Psalm 89:6, 7, "For who in the skies can be compared to the Lord? Who among the heavenly beings is like the Lord, a God feared in the council of the holy ones, great and terrible above all that are round about him?" I accept the apocalyptic literature view that Satan is a disobedient servant, a prodigal son, and an angel who fell and was cast out of heaven (Revelation 12:9). I accept the view that he now operates a cunning opposition program. He guides a revolting kingdom of evil.

I do not seek to answer the question that stumped the Sadducees, Just when did Satan fall? Nor do I worry about the questions which perplex some of my African friends: How do the ancestral spirits of those who were evil align themselves with Satan's efforts? Are they now acting as demons?

I prefer to concentrate on the reasons I am certain Satan's power is limited, and to reflect upon what that means for me.

Satan is necessarily limited because God is so supremely sovereign. I find, both in my own experience and in reading from many sources, that the higher my own view of God, the lower I will see the "opposition party," Satan and the demons. Both the poetic and the

apocalyptic literature of the Scriptures agree in this
assumption.

Satan is limited because he is finally only a creature,
apparently unable to repent, and aware already of his
final and total defeat. He knows that his time is short,
that his rebellion against the Almighty is doomed to fail,
and that believers can defeat him by being "wise as to
what is good and guileless as to what is evil" (Romans
16:19). The Apostle Paul promised the converts at Rome
that, if this is true of them, "then the God of peace will
soon crush Satan under your feet" (Romans 16:20).

Satan is limited by God's mighty acts and provisions
for His people. In Exodus No. 1 God rescued His people
from Pharaoh; in Exodus No. 2 He came in His Son and
led out His new people, the church. Devout Pharisees
believed that the law God gave at the Exodus was God's
safeguard against all the demons of all the nations round
about. Satan is mentioned only three times in all the
thirty-nine books of the Old Testament (Job 1,
1 Chronicles 21:1, and Zechariah 3:1, 2). When all the
world becomes the throne room of God Almighty,
Satan finds "No Trespassing" signs automatically set
against him at every doorway.

Satan is limited because God's Son came as the
stronger Man and bound him. The Seed of the woman
has been here, in a mighty Christ-event, and has done a
deed which divided all history into two, bruising the
serpent's head. Jesus Christ, by His victorious life,
death, and resurrection has made victory possible for
the weakest believer, and forever set Satan's limits and
curbed his powers.

Satan is limited by every person's free will, by decisions which Satan cannot coerce, by one's ability to say "no" to the devil and "yes" to God. The Essenes and John the Baptist saw their baptism of repentance as a massive and total acceptance of God's way and will and a total turning from all of the demonic injustice, corruption, and sin of the times.

In corroboration of man's repentance, the Essenes believed God acted to free the baptized one "from the wrath to come" (Matthew 3:7). It is almost as if baptism immunized the person from Satanic attack. When God and man together act against Satan's efforts, there is little Satan can do.[1]

Although I believe that Satan is radically limited, I do not go along with those who see Satan limited to chaos, to the void, to negation, to nothingness. I do not equate him with the air, with nonbeing. I do not agree with those who see in Satan only the projection of their own dark side. I do not feel that Satan is only a myth like Nirvana, or the *neti-neti* of Brahmanism, nor that his only dominion is over boredom, ennui, fatigue, and stupor. I think Freud was wrong (as usual) when he said, "The devil is nothing but repressed anal impulses."

I do feel that both of God's victories, Exodus No. I and Exodus No. 2, through Moses and through Christ, have rolled back the principalities and powers. Even when evil dwells in structured, impersonal systems, they are still part of God's creation (Colossians 1:16). Even though they are holding persons captive who walk in disobedience to God (Ephesians 2:2), yet these evil systems are repeatedly being outwitted and circumvented by God's power. Pharaoh or Pilate may intend to harass, but God overrules for good.

Christ disarmed the evil systems by His death
(Colossians 2:15). Christ taunts the principalities and
powers by what He is able to do through His apparently
weak church (Ephesians 3:10). Christ sees to it that the
powers cannot go too far in harassing Christians
(Romans 8:38, 39), and Christ will eventually destroy
alien powers altogether.

Demonic forces like Nazism and Communism shrink
to mere ideologies. To the eyes of faith and in the
experience of Christians, demonic rulers like the king of
Tyre shrink to ordinary men. Mammon shrinks to
necessary finances. The deified state shrinks to a government under God's sovereignty. Patriotic citizens are
seen as people not significantly different from those of
other countries.[2]

Satan is limited in what he can do to me because of
God's image within me. God's image within me has no
affinity with Satan and his wiles. There is even some re-
vulsion. I know I am fallen, and my baser desires have
an almost unlimited tendency toward self-centeredness
and sin. But God's image within me is not effaced, not
destroyed, and not rendered impotent.

Satan is limited by the parameters of a providential,
loving, overruling God who is actively arranging my life.
God is working all things together for my good, if I am
one who loves Him and is seeking to do His will. The
rays of God's loving purposes for my life are radiating
out toward all of my life-space with more than radioac-
tive power. I am enveloped by God's love rays and surrounded by them. True I am often ornery and rebellious,
but God's love is always there.

Satan is limited by the powerful effect of the intercessory prayers of Christians who are praying for me. Satan complained that he found a hedge around Job, making it hard to get at him to hurt or harass him. I believe that the loving prayers of my wife, my family, my house-fellowship group, some of my faculty colleagues who pray for me daily, and others the Holy Spirit prompts to pray for me, are a mystical but very real protection. I believe that "the effectual fervent prayer of a righteous man availeth much" (James 5:16, KJV) and that one of prayer's benefits is precisely to limit what Satan can do to seduce or to harass me.

I believed this as a child. Later in my doctoral studies in psychology of religion I read widely in parapsychology, in extrasensory perception, mental telepathy, clairvoyance, and the mystical reaches of the mind. I have tried to keep informed about the continuing research in these areas. I am convinced that the mystical powers of the human mind are fantastic. My childlike faith in the power of prayer has been reaffirmed by personal experience, by an increasing knowledge of God, and further research into the grandeur of the human mind.

For Additional Reading and Reference:

Davis, John H. *Contemporary Counterfeits* (Winona Lake: BMH Books, 1973).

De Haan, Richard W. *Satan, Satanism, and Witchcraft* (Grand Rapids: Zondervan, 1972).

Kallas, James. *The Real Satan* (Minneapolis: Augsburg, 1975).

Lewis, C. S. *The Screwtape Letters* (New York: Macmillan, 1959).

Lhermitte, Jean. *Diabolical Possession, True and False* (Westminster, Md.: Christian Classics, 1963).
Richards, John. *But Deliver Us from Evil* (New York: Seabury Press, 1974).
Richardson, Carl. *Exorcism: New Testament Style* (Old Tappan, N.J.: Revell, 1974).

3
God Tests Me
to Strengthen Me

The Scriptures teach that untested virtue is not really a strong virtue, that untested innocence is not so much faith as perhaps mere credulity. There is no other way to develop spiritual muscle than by resisting opposition and seduction. A person cannot learn to distinguish between good and evil without ever being confronted by evil. Loving fathers teach and discipline their children to help them learn right living. God also tests His children to strengthen them, but always in a loving act as when He gave His Son. Believers need this perspective in their philosophy of life, but I find it sadly missing in much of the "deliverance ministry" literature.

It was a tragedy that Eve saw only Satan's seduction and not a loving God's testing. If she had been able to hear her loving Creator testing her, asking her to use her freedom wisely and responsibly, inviting her to develop discernment, challenging her to use her head and to think through her values, her loyalties, her limits, her rebellions—she could not so readily have alibied, "The devil made me do it!" She would have been wiser to ponder the influences of God's Holy Spirit, and not only those of the unholy spirit, in deciding freely her own course of action.

It was tragic that Adam saw only a dear friend's seduction and not a testing by His God. If he could have seen it as God's testing, God's invitation to grow up, God's way for him to grow strong by using his powers of will and thought, Adam could not have alibied, "The woman made me do it!" Why did he seem to assume she was fully responsible, but he was less so because "she did it first." The group dynamics researchers have invented a fancy name for the assumption that the initiator is more guilty than the imitator. They call it "magical exculpation."

The biblical emphasis—that God's people should see God's loving testing much more than the devil's tempting—comes through emphatically in the story of Job. Even though Satan was tempting and attacking him, Job talked about God's testing which He was allowing. Even Job's worldly friends, with their limited perspective, knew better than to look first for the devil in the situation. Testing and suffering are crucial times to learn about God's ways, His providences, and the uses He makes of adversity.

Job's wife has been accused of poor attitudes and limited vision. But even she didn't get involved in naming Job's demons. She suggested that Job address God about his situation and testings. Job kept doing this, and learned about God's compassion, God's mercy, God's sovereignty in His world, and God's infinite holiness. It is doubtful if Job would have learned all this if he had focused on Satan who was attacking him.

The psalmist echoed the biblical emphasis upon

God's testing rather than the devil's tempting. He knew he was in trouble. He was oppressed and he was distressed, but he kept talking directly to God. He kept asking God to carry through His testing of him, His judging of him, His teaching of him, His strengthening of him, and His delivering of him. Not once did the psalmist alibi, "The devil made me do it!"

When the psalmist resorted to naming demons at all, they were "enemies," by which he meant wicked people, his pursuers, the evildoer, the fool, or his adversaries.

The Prophet Habakkuk must have caught some of the truth that adversity might be accepted as a testing of God which was good for him. He cried, "Though the fig tree do not blossom, nor fruit be on the vines, the produce of the olive fail and the fields yield no food, the flock be cut off from the fold and there be no herd in the stalls, yet I will rejoice in the Lord, I will joy in the God of my salvation" (Habakkuk 3:17, 18).

A classic instance of one event which was both God's testing and Satan's tempting was David's desire to number Israel. When the incident was first reported in 2 Samuel 24:1, it was clearly asserted that the Lord Himself was testing David by inciting him to number Israel. Jehovah's act, and only Jehovah's act, was discussed.

God had explicitly commanded His people to allow Himself alone to be their King, to depend upon Him and His "holy war" deliverances for their victory, and to accept His Word through the prophet to guide them. Through Samuel God warned against relying instead upon the way of earthly kings with their armies, chariots, and human warfare. Jehovah had acted to set the standards and pleaded with Israel to obey them.

Israel went against God's plea through Samuel and got David as king, fortunately a fairly good leader. God wanted to test King David's heart, to see whether he would rely on God's deliverance through "holy war," shouting the victory shout, and waiting upon God to scatter the enemy. Or would King David go the way of neighboring worldly-wise kings and rely instead upon the size of his army? Numbering Israel, to see how many potential soldiers he had, was a crucial parting of the ways. God asked for a choice. God Himself was testing His servant.

Several hundred years later, after Israel had lost much of her monotheism and had been sadly influenced by the polytheism of the neighboring pagans, a later writer tells the same story (1 Chronicles 21:1). Now God's testing of David is seen only as Satan's tempting! This tragic shift in viewpoint happens when faith in God is low. Then it's easy to say, "The devil made me do it."

God's people have lost something very precious when they no longer see God always in control, allowing them to be tested for their own good and to strengthen them, even during seductive circumstances. If God's people can see their God trusting them, allowing Satan to touch their bodies, as in Job's case, because God believes they will come through victoriously, then God's people will not quickly say, "The devil made me do it."

The biblical way of reporting the "God-is-testing-but-Satan-is-tempting" dilemma emphasizes how wise the person is who keeps his or her attention on God's testing.

Obviously Christ had His mind on His Father's will,

even when Satan was attacking. Satan tried to seduce Him through fleshly appetite, or by a desire for magic, or by offering to exempt Him from what human flesh is heir to, or by suggesting the benefits of power and prestige. But Jesus was hearing this as a test of whether or not He really valued dialogue with His Father, hearing the words proceeding out of His mouth, more than anything else in all the world. Jesus was sensitive to His Father's will about His life, His worship, His way of service. He was learning obedience and strength through what He was suffering. It was still the Father's testing more than Satan's tempting. He soon spelled out His responses more fully in the Sermon on the Mount.

Even though the Apostle Paul knew that his "thorn in the flesh" was a Satanic attack, Paul refused to address Satan, to get his friends to name the demon and exorcise it, or even to discuss Satan's wiles in his life. Paul talked to God about it in prayer. He besought the Lord repeatedly in intense petition.

By keeping his attention upon the testing God was doing he learned how God perfects His strength even in weakness. This is the profound incarnational principle by which Almighty God has chosen to work in a finite and limited world. Paul received private tutoring in one of the profoundest mysteries of the entire faith.

Because he chose to keep pondering God's testing (in Satan's thorn in the flesh) Paul learned how to glory in infirmity. He learned how to claim the power of God to compensate for a weakness. He learned how God allows a weakness or handicap to come to some to whom He gives abundance of revelations. God doesn't want His finest servants ruined with a swelled head.

I believe it is good to keep pointing out to Christians that two things are happening in their lives through one traumatic event. God wants to strengthen them through suffering, even though Satan is in it too, tempting. Paul reminded the Corinthian congregation that God was testing them through the presence of an incestuous brother to see whether they would have courage to insist upon holy living in the church.

But Paul warned them not to be ignorant of Satan's devices. "He will try to get his horns in it too," would be a free translation. "Don't let Satan discourage the repentant brother by waiting a little too long to confirm your love to him. Lick Satan by forgiving the repentant person promptly and restoring him quickly," Paul is saying. "Beware lest the testing and refining God is doing is missed, and only the failure and loss Satan is seeking is realized!"

If God is really the only God, and He is fully sovereign and in control, then I will give first attention, fullest attention, and longest attention to what He may be trying to say to me, before I turn to see what the tempter, fallen angel, subtle beast, seducer, and accuser may be up to.

The Epistles of Peter contain thorough discussions of sufferings, oppressions, distresses, attacks, and the like which harass the Christian. But, like Job in the Old Testament, the Petrine Epistles mention satanic attack last and least. Suffering is first surveyed to see what God in His testings may be doing. Suffering can be within the will of God. As Christ's were, so the Christians sufferings can be redemptive. Suffering can purify character, and as such should be embraced cheerfully. Suffering in

God's cause can bring glory to God. Suffering so severe
that it might destroy will be brief.

Only after a thorough consideration of God's testings,
does Peter mention briefly Satan as a roaring lion going
about seeking whom he may destroy. The proportion
and balance of Peter's approach is still the wise way for
the church.

The persons who endure God's testings, and learn
obedience through suffering, become God's mighty
ones, persons He uses. God often reverses the usual
hierarchical and over-under roles and structures which
men set up. He entrusts the underdog with testing, suffering, and then with moral responsibility for leadership.
By the suffering which God allows, He produces His
saints and His mighty men.

It was from his unfair suffering, patiently borne, that
God raised up Joseph to power and influence amongst
world empires. It was from injustice and a despised
place in life that God prepared Queen Esther and Mor-
decai for crucial tasks. They would have missed a great
deal in life if they had grown embittered and launched
tirades against the devil.

Because Daniel and the three Hebrew youths could
face testing with courage, and did not cringe or grow
angry or violent under injustice, God could use them to
witness for him in high places.

In the New Testament *"Haustafeln"* (household rules)
passages like Colossians 3:18—4:1, Ephesians 5:21—6:9,
and 1 Peter 2:13—3:7 the apostles repeatedly appealed
to the suffering underdog to offer moral leadership.
More appeals were directed to the slave for moral
leadership than were directed to the slave owner. More

appeals were directed to the subordinate wives than to the head-of-the-home husbands. More appeals were made to children than to parents.[1]

God disciplines those He loves and He chastens His choicest children (Hebrews 12:3-11). So I can know that God's testing is never with the intent that I fail. God's testing is vastly different from temptation. "Let no one say when he is tempted, 'I am tempted by God'; for God cannot be tempted with evil and he himself tempts no one" (James 1:13).

God takes no delight in seeing me sin, in seeing me weakened, and in seeing me fall. He is faithful and will not allow me to be tested above what I am able to bear. He knows my frame. He restrains the tension and the testing to my strength limits so that I can conquer it, bear it, grow from it, mature by it, and become a better person.

The surplus I would not have been able to stand, God refuses to allow Satan to introduce. He provides the way to escape so I can bear it, come through victoriously, and feel good about myself afterward. Even when I foolishly overestimate my strength, and begin to sink like Peter walking on the water, He comes quickly to my rescue. We never have the right to say, "I couldn't avoid sinning. I was overpowered. The devil made me do it."

For Additional Reading and Reference

Frankl, Victor E. *Man's Search for Meaning* (New York: Washington Square Press, 1968).

Hulme, William. *Dialogue with Despair* (New York: Abingdon Press, 1968).

Ikin, A. Graham. *Victory over Suffering* (Great Neck,

N.Y.: Channel Press, 1961).

Kelsey, Morton. *Encounter with God.* (Minneapolis: Bethany Fellowship, 1972).

Nouwen, Henri. *The Wounded Healer: Ministry in Contemporary Society* (New York: Doubleday, 1972).

Oates, Wayne E. *Anxiety in Christian Experience* (Waco: Word, 1971).

———. *The Revelation of God in Human Suffering* (Philadelphia: Westminster Press).

Weatherhead, Leslie D. *Why Do Men Suffer—* (New York: Abingdon Press).

Wolf, William J. *No Cross No Crown* (New York: Doubleday, 1957).

Yoder, John H. *The Politics of Jesus* (Grand Rapids: Eerdmans, 1972).

4
The Bible Warns Me of Satan's Snares

The wise man in the Book of Proverbs says, "In vain is a net spread in the sight of any bird" (1:17). The Scriptures do expose the devil's dirty tricks. Recent reports from the Satan worshipers, and experimenters with the occult, are enough to warn anyone. Truly those persons ensnared by Satan are made to suffer horribly.

The snares the devil uses have been laid bare in the Scriptures. These things are written for my admonition and learning. I read holy history as my history. These people were as fully human as I am. Their temptations and failures are not whitewashed. No Watergate conspirators have tried to alter the tapes or the records. I can see Satan's favorite tricks. He has to set his snares for my feet while I watch him do it.

Furthermore, I not only can see his objectives, but I can calmly study his strategies. I am not left ignorant of his devices. His methods are set forth in all of their variety. I have every chance to "catch him at it" when he tries his methods against me.

I can analyze the way he uses my basic God-given desires, and appeals to them. I am no longer in the dark regarding the subtle power of his suggestions. The more I learn from the various schools of psychology about the depth motivations of human beings, the more Satan's methods, appeals, and cunning make sense.

Holy history, as set forth with such vivid honesty in the Scriptures, allows me to monitor the inner struggles and the feelings of a David who has committed adultery, a Judas who has decided to betray, a Jacob who has cheated, a Peter who has lied, or a Saul-Paul who has succumbed to legalism. These glimpses of the anguish of the soul forewarn me.

I am forewarned that I give place to the devil if I allow the sun to go down upon my wrath (Ephesians 4:26). I am inviting him in. My denied feelings and muttered resentments open wide the door.

Anger not worked through is heavy, shameful, and hard to think about. So I push unforgiven anger and unreconciled wrath down out of my conscious awareness and try to think about something else. Amusements, sports, travel, excitement, new interests can all help me to "forget." I refuse to take ownership of my real feelings, to admit that those angers are really me. I let the sun go down on them, night after night in denial, until they seem like "not-me" anymore. The "real me" again seems like a friendly, loving person, and the unreconciled wrath and hardened malice forced down into my unconscious seems far away, something I can disown.

Into that disowned "not-me" of frozen anger Satan comes. I am truly a split personality. I am "possessed." I feel anxious. I show symptoms of strain, sickness, disorder in my emotions or my body. I erupt in irrational anger over little things which should not make me mad. Or I feel recurring depression, despair, and worthlessness until I think of suicide.

I am possessed by a "demon." Yes, but no one will really help me who merely discerns that I have a demon called "anger," names it, and casts it out with an exorcist ritual. It matters little whether the exorcist flourishes the crucifix and uses holy water, or keeps mentioning "the blood" or the "name of Jesus."

I am truly helped only when I recover my ability to take ownership of that anger, to admit who I am mad at, and to take responsible steps to be reconciled and to make restitution. I have "named the demon" when I have taken responsibility for my wrath, refused the cop-out of saying, "The devil made me do it," and when I have followed the active way of repentance and faith outlined in Matthew 18 and elsewhere in the Scriptures.

I am also forewarned in this Bible that my "acquisitive instinct," my love of money which is a source of all kinds of evil, can make me give place to the devil. God has cautioned me again and again that a disciple can betray for thirty pieces of silver, a dedicated donor can lie about his generosity and actually keep back some of the money he pretends to give, a smart farmer can ignore the poor so as to get rich more quickly.

Satan's cunning ways of using my love of money and possessions to control and ruin me are described vividly in the case study of Job. Satan knows that God often blesses the honest and godly farmer. Satan may suggest that if I live that way I too will get rich. I may begin to tithe so that my chickens will lay more eggs, and so that God will bless my business. Satan knows that I can slowly but surely be seduced away from serving God because I love Him and believe His kingdom is best for me and everyone else. He can get me to serve God for the fringe benefits themselves, out of smart self-interest, because it pays well for me.

Satan has seen the love of money and possessions become god in people's lives so many times that he is willing to gamble on it working every time. "You've blessed Job," he taunts God, "but take away his possessions and he will curse You to Your face." Satan can fill the heart of a devout Ananias so that he lies to the Holy Ghost and is stricken dead. Satan gloats in the power of the temptation to materialism, love of money, and pride in possessions.

A well-meaning exorcist or deliverance minister trying to solve the entire problem, once and for all, in one fell swoop is not likely to help much. The New Testament epistles record no such futile attempt.

As I read my own situation and temptations written large in the lives of Bible characters, and try to learn the enduring ways of victory over the demonic lure of riches, I observe several things. I will be wise if I invite God to test me by adversity, if need be, to help reset my heart's affections upon Him alone. Hopefully, I can say with Job, "Though he slay me, yet will I trust in him" (13:15, KJV). But I dare not glide down the road of selfish materialism and then disclaim responsibility by saying, "The devil made me do it."

I can keep my natural instinct to acquire from becoming a satanic inroad and seduction if I keep my stewardship and giving open to review. I can allow trusted brothers and sisters to examine what I am doing with my money until two of them can conscientiously countersign my budget. Ananias would not have succumbed to Satan so readily if he had done this as he was selling his land and bringing his offering to the church meeting. It may be that my individual conscience is too fallible and too easily seduced by greed for me to be making stewardship decisions alone, without brotherly admonition. According to 1 Timothy 6:17-19 I am entitled to being warned, during church services, against setting my hope on riches.

I believe I can gain strength for victory over the devil's ploy of love of money if I deliberately keep aware of the needs of the poor. The rich man who opened his eyes in hell should have spent more time talking with the poor beggars who lay at his gate. Like the good Samaritan I need to pour out my life, money, and energy for the poor man robbed on the Jericho road, but I also have some responsibility to work toward justice so the road becomes safe from robbers.

If I admit my sheer inability to really live unless I know I am being addressed by the living God, I will be better able to refuse to try to live by bread alone, by materialism. I can live in an attitude of worship, constantly tuned to what God would tell me. This will help counteract Satan's seductive suggestion that I live only for materialism, devoting my powers merely to making earth's stones into bread. Genuine worship can guard me against the snare of technology.

The Bible also warns that Satan will seduce me into desiring to be an exception from that to which human flesh is heir. Subtly Satan suggests that I can become a super person, going up the holy mount, then into the holy city, and inside the holy temple, and then to the top of its holy pinnacle. With my spiritual expertness I can now perform stunts for the praise and admiration of onlookers. Others may stub their toes if they are foolish enough to jump down from great heights, but I can be the exception. God really owes me special protection because I'm such an important and extra religious person. I can feed my own ego and vanity and become a very powerful person spiritually. I can glorify God and yet collect an awful lot of glory for myself. Satan can quote Scriptures to me to prove why I should "claim the promises of God," and be the exception.

The way to defeat Satan in this strategy is to refuse to "tempt the Lord your God." This was the answer of Jesus (Matthew 4:7).

To insure victory over the devil I may need to accept supervision in my work in the church, asking my supervisor to look with me, as piercingly and honestly as he can, at my reasons for doing what I am doing in Christian service. A good supervisor will insist that I declare my goals and objectives, and show how my activities are designed to reach them. He will look with me at my efforts, helping me appraise how useful they really are to others, and how many are actually self-serving. He will be painfully frank with me if he sees me merely doing stunts to get attention. He will expose my fraud if I am misusing Scriptures to cover up my pride.

Genuine "discipling the brother" sessions, when fellow Christians give me feedback on how they see me, and admonish me on ways to improve, will help me withstand Satan's offer of some kingdom and glory if I will only stoop to take his way.

The seduction to pride is tricky business, and has often confused well-meaning Christians. Some set out to conquer pride by overemphasizing "crucifying the self," focusing on our unworthiness, and stressing what miserable wretches everyone really is. A generation of Christians sang, "Would He devote that sacred head for such a worm as I?"

The trouble with the wormy, self-crucifying, self-despising, and hair-shirt way of combating pride is that it fails one of two ways, each equally bad. Either it fails because the person becomes proud once more, proud of being such a humble person, proud of being more self-despising than anyone else, and proud of being more spiritual than anyone else. Or, if the self-despising really succeeds, the person loses self-respect, becomes a shrinking and apologetic nobody, a failure who apologizes for existing. Bruce Larson, in his book *The One and Only You,* urges that persons build their self-respect by "discovering your past, living in your present, claiming your future, enjoying your strengths, all as a person known by God."

The goal is a wholesome self-respect, and a realistic love of self as a unique person God has made. He first loved us, worthy or not. God's love teaches us to value and love ourselves for the image of God we bear and for the infinite value God sees in us. Each person is one of a kind, possessing a combination of gifts different from anyone else who has ever lived.

We are to love our neighbors as we love ourselves. If we can only value and love ourselves as a worm, all our relationships will be wormy too. But we can hold our heads erect before God and man, glad to be a unique person whom God can use. Our feeling of self-worth can be kept from becoming ingrown, self-centered pride if we use our abilities to serve others in love.

There is much that we can do to help fellow Christians from straying after Satan, as Paul puts it in 1 Timothy 5:15. Paul feared that a widow, unloved and cared for by the congregation might lapse into gadding about and idle gossip (1 Timothy 5:13). If the congregation failed her, she would be open to Satan's seduction into a life of idle gossip.

But the solution here, as everywhere else where Satan's seduction of a member is mentioned in the epistles, is for the church to meet the member's needs in a vital congregational life. There is no hint that an exorcism service be held for the widow who strayed after Satan. If I am a member of a congregation which includes such a person, I need to see that a real program of mutual aid and responsible ministry is arranged so that the widow's needs are met. The Bible forewarns me about this method Satan uses to snare widows, and I am responsible to help in a practical, down-to-earth way.

Paul warned that a recent convert, if given leadership responsibility too soon, "may be puffed up with conceit and fall into the condemnation of the devil" (1 Timothy 3:6). The way of victory here, as in so many cases where the devil is mentioned, is wise prevention.

I am not ignorant of this device of Satan. I simply refuse to ordain a novice. I insist that leaders have time for training and apprenticeship. I apply good common sense. I allow the recent convert to mature with years and experience.

There is nothing eerie, awesome, or mysterious about

assisting a friend in victory over the devil. The wiles which the devil uses turn out to be the very human desires of conceit, pride, laziness, ambition, desire to acquire, desire for power, and the like.

God's people, Israel, were not troubled by demonism or exorcism because of their high monotheism, and their conviction that God Jehovah was so high, so sovereign, so omnipotent that beside Him there really was no other god at all. Yet they were sternly warned to have nothing to do with the pagan deities. They were to keep completely away from Baal worship. They were to have nothing to do with magic, magicians, and Satan's devices. See Leviticus 20:27 and many such passages.

For Additional Reading and Reference:

Breeze, Dave. *His Infernal Majesty* (Chicago: Moody Press, 1974).

Collins, Gary R. *Overcoming Anxiety* (Wheaton: Key Publishers, 1973).

Cruz, Nicky. *Satan on the Loose* (Old Tappan, N.J.: Revell, 1973).

Koch, Kurt E. *Occult Bondage and Deliverance: Advice for Counseling the Sick, the Troubled, and the Occulty Oppressed* (West Germany: Evangelical Press).

Larson, Bruce. *The One and Only You* (Waco: Word Books, 1974).

McCall, T. S., and Levitt, Zola. *Satan in the Sanctuary* (Chicago: Moody Press, 1973).

Nicola, John J. *Diabolical Possession and Exorcism* (Rockford, Ill: Tan Books, 1974).

Sanders, J. Oswald. *Satan Is No Myth* (Chicago: Moody Press, 1975).

Southard, Samuel. *Anger in Love* (Philadelphia: Westminster Press, 1973).

Unger, Merrill. *Demons in the World Today* (Wheaton: Tyndale, 1971, 1972).

Warnke, Mike. *The Satan Seller* (Plainfield, N.J.: Logos, 1972).

5
A Way of Victory Is Always Available

People may be feeling they have demons because they sense that so many things are terribly wrong in the world, and yet nobody seems able to repent and make restitution for anything. Almost all honest persons have been sickened by wrongs done to slaves, to Indians, to the poor, to the aged, to other nations, to minorities, to draft dodgers, to the mentally ill, and to aborted babies. The sheer inability to make restitution may be raising people's guilt level and resulting in naming demons in one another. This possibility is suggested by a lifelong educator of psychiatrists, Karl Menninger, in his book, *Whatever Became of Sin?*

Aldous Huxley in his *Devils of London* suggests that demons increase "when people feel the unfeelable feelings for which there are no thinkable thoughts or doable deeds."

Such vague explanations don't help me much. I long for some "handles" to take hold of, some practical suggestions on where to turn for victory.

The Jews gave themselves decisively to Jehovah, to be His people and to trust His keeping in absolutely every area of their lives. Because of this, they were able to take some of the practices which their superstitious, fear-ridden neighbors were using as exorcistic rites to get rid of demons, and to assign faith meanings to them.

Whereas superstitious neighbors used bells on their horses to ward off demons, God's people used them to praise God while they plowed God's earth. Bells on high priest's robes took on a new meaning (Exodus 28:33-35). Incense was given a different meaning (Leviticus 16:12, 13). Smearing blood on lintels and doorposts (Exodus 12:7, 13), and the wearing of phylactories (Deuteronomy 6:6-8) were assigned meanings appropriate to the worship of the one sovereign God, whose power was so supreme and sublime that His people rarely mentioned demons and had no rituals to exorcise them.

There is no reason for God's people to fear thirteen floors, flying saucers, or black cats, or for them to dabble in levitation, powwowing, palm reading, or water witching.

God's people should refuse to over-personalize nature or human nature and powers that are hard to understand. When King Saul started to act strangely his people did not say, "The devil has sent a demon into you and we will exorcise you by a ritual of adjuration!" They said, "Behold now, an evil spirit from God is tormenting you," and they suggested "music therapy." They got a young man, David, to come and play for him on his harp. The narrative concludes with the happy report that "whenever the evil spirit from God was upon Saul, David took the lyre and played it with his hand; so Saul was refreshed, and was well, and the evil spirit departed from him." (See 1 Samuel 16:14-23.) This is Old Testament exorcism, practically the only case of the entire Bible from which Jesus and the apostles read.

I am impressed in the biblical stories, with how many simple, honest, earnest solutions are given to problems persons were having with the devil. But the solution was never an exorcistic ritual.

When Satan desired Peter so that he might sift him as wheat as Christ warned (Luke 22:31), what was actually done to give Peter victory? Christ gave him a warning, a piecing look of reminder; a maiden gave him a confronting question; and Peter's conscience did the rest. Victory came by Peter's act of repentance and new steps of faith.

Paul warned that a person who tried to serve as pastor but who was not well thought of by outsiders, might fall into the snare and reproach of the devil (1 Timothy 3:6, 7). But Paul hinted of no magical, mysterious prevention beforehand nor any exorcistic cure after the tragedy had occurred. The implication seems to be simply that the church should not ask anyone to be pastor who is not already well thought of by outsiders. The discouragements and handicaps would be so severe that, through it all, he might be snared by the enemy. So, don't do it.

Satan hindered Paul from going to visit the congregation of Thessalonica as he was determined to do. The desire grew more intense and the hindering more traumatic. It happened again and again. Finally, it reached a crisis point when Paul declared he "could bear it no longer!" He found victory in deciding to allow a trusted friend to run the errand for him. He merely became willing to be left behind at Athens alone, and sent his friend Timothy in his place. It was as simple as that. (See 1 Thessalonians 2:17-20 and 3:1-5.)

The word of wisdom to me from this story is that if I am stymied and blocked by what seems to be inhuman forces of opposition, I should always have a strong Timothy-type person whom I can ask to do an end run for me. As a halfback carries the football around the end, so a Timothy can team up with me to get past satanic blockage. Naturally I also want to be available to be a Timothy, and to serve my brother or sister in the same way if they experience a stalemate.

I prick up my ears when James, the brother of the Lord Jesus, starts giving instructions on how to resist the devil (James 4:1-10). But again I find nothing esoteric or mysterious that demands the services of an itinerant exorcist.

James calls first for a frank realization that our troubles come from within ourselves, from the passions which war in our members. He leaves no room for the alibi, "The devil made me do it."

James stresses taking our place decisively with God's people, knowing that friendship with the world is enmity with God. Many people would have less trouble with the devil if they changed the gang they run around with.

James asks me to examine my heart for pride, since God yearns jealously over the image of God He gave me. He points to the ambivalence we all feel between a wholesome pride, the self-respect we all need, and the God-defying pride which made Lucifer fall.

James asks for decisive obedience to what I feel God is asking me to do (and he quotes Abraham offering up his son Isaac). He asks for a strong monotheism, the belief that there is only one God, and points out the demon problems when monotheism is too low. He sees

demons themselves characterized by shuddering ambivalence—trembling in indecision. James calls for positive commitment, for life-and-death earnestness with
God, for decisiveness. These are the antidote to demons.

When James gets around to discussing bodily sickness
and distress (the subject which so often brings on the
suggestion that a demon be exorcized) he mentions Job,
whose sickness was reported as satanic oppression and
attack (Job 1). But James pointedly omits any suggestion that believers should assume that suffering is an attack of Satan. Rather he cites the prophets as great sufferers and stresses the valuable patience they learned
from God's testing.

Most exorcistic rituals include the words, "I adjure
you by Jesus," or, "I command you in the name of
Jesus," but James forbids swearing, adjuration, or oath
(James 5:12).

I understand James to say that life's cheerful
experiences and life's sicknesses should be shared in the
church fellowship; that prayer is the supreme resource
when sickness strikes; that the local congregational
elders (not itinerant exorcists) are the ones to call; that
the best of medicine, as symbolized by oil, and the
strongest of prayer should be utilized by the congregation to benefit the sick member; that confession to one
another should flow freely; and that patient waiting for
answers to prayer—like Elijah practiced—should be the
accepted pattern (James 5:13-18).

I understand James to say that I should acknowledge
ownership and responsibility for my bodily lusts. He
does not suggest that I disguise them by renaming them
demons, and wait for some expert to deliver me.

James urges me to seek spiritual renewal through the experience, demonstrating the new nature of being created in God's own likeness (James 1:18). He cautions me to cut out the superlatives, the strong talk, the clamor, or the slander (James 3:8). He advises that I seek forgiveness for my inevitable share of the blame and the wrong. As I open my heart to receive forgiveness, it becomes easier to allow that same forgiveness to flow through me to others.

Paul warns that I really give place to the devil when I repress my anger and let the sun go down on unreconciled wrath. Instead of repressing it so as to invite depression, or merely expressing it in evil talk coming out of my mouth, Paul suggests how I can process my anger realistically, maturely, and for the good of everyone. (See Ephesians 4:25-32.)

All the way through my anger episode, while I am refusing to repress it and thus give place to the devil, and while I am processing it by mutual forgiveness between myself and the offender, Paul urges me to be checking out with God's indwelling Spirit everything I do and say so I do not grieve Him.

[handwritten marginal notes:]
① Be careful to use only helpful edifying words.
② Get rid of all anger, bitterness, + passion
③ Don't stay angry all day. Instead be kind hearted.
④ Do not make God's spirit sad.

For Additional Reading and Reference:

Bjornstad, James, and Johnson, Shildes. *Stars, Signs, and Salvation in the Age of Aquarius* (Minneapolis: Bethany Fellowship, 1971).

Boisen, Anton B. *The Exploration of the Inner World* (Philadelphia: University of Pennsylvania Press, 1971).

Delling, Gerhard. *Worship in the New Testament* (Philadelphia: Westminster Press, 1962).

Freeman, Hobart E. *Angels of Light* (Plainfield, N. J.: Logos, 1971).

Glasser, William. *Reality Therapy* (New York: Harper & Row, 1965).

Kelly, Henry A. *The Devil, Demonology, and Witchcraft: The Development of Christian Beliefs in Evil Spirits* (New York: Doubleday, 1974).

Kildahl, John P. *The Psychology of Speaking in Tongues* (New York: Harper & Row, 1972).

Tozer, A. W. *I Talk Back to the Devil* (Harrisburg, Pa.: Christian Publications, 1972).

West, R. Frederick. *Light Beyond Shadows* (New York: Macmillan, 1959).

6
I Don't Have to Fear Demons

The demons of the animists are horribly real to them. Voodoo spells kill people. Idols, the dwelling place of demons, are potent in the lives of persons who believe that many gods exist and must be appeased. The scholarly name for this view is "metaphysical dualism."[1]

I have personally observed some of the sad, startling, agonized "attacks" which many of the writers on exorcism describe in great detail. Persons have been brought to me for help after exorcists had worked on them. I have seen people "flat out" or violent. But I choose not to recount startling stories, because they prove nothing.

I believe, with the Apostle Paul, that the nature of demons makes it extremely important that I don't cater to them. Paul warned the Corinthian Christians sternly, "I do not want you to be partners with demons. . . . You cannot partake of the table of the Lord and the table of demons" (1 Corinthians 10:20, 21). I will not deliberately invest myself, my time, my energy, or my powers in any cooperation with those relying upon magic, the occult, or the like.

But then Paul just as firmly insists that, for him, idol-demons have no reality. He almost shouts, "Do I imply then . . . that an idol is anything? No." (1 Corinthians 10:19). He had thundered this affirmation earlier, as a Christian confession of faith, in 1 Corinthians 8:4, "We know that 'an idol [or the demon it enshrines] has no real existence,' and that 'there is no God but one.' "

I want to avoid any subtle feeling of superiority toward the animists, even as I assert that the Christian faith provides a better way. I agree with Middleton and Winter when they say that Western missionaries failed to show how Christian faith deals with ultimate causes, and so many animists continued looking to their tribal witch doctors to "explain" misfortune, the spirit world, and how to take some decisive action amidst life's trauma and uncertainties.[2]

Anthropological studies of witchcraft in tribes in many diverse cultures reveal that "possessed" people, witches, and sorcerers often are the scapegoats of society. They epitomize the standardized nightmares of their culture.

The behavior of witches provides an outlet for massive rage or grief in their system of culture. The fear generated around witches helps to enforce the basic standards and taboos of the society and socially accepted behavior. When both missionaries and colonial governments forbade witchcraft and sorcery, the animists saw this opposition to their attempt to deal with evil as an alignment with the forces of evil. Apparently many of them totally misinterpreted the intention of the missionary.

As Christians from Western rationalized and scientized cultures mingle with new Christians from backgrounds of animism, we must explore as never before what we really believe about ancestral spirits, unexplainable sufferings, and discarnate spirits. We have shied away from these issues too long. We need to clarify our convictions concerning the ultimate anxieties of persons and about personalized evil.

Every Christian is entitled and called to live without fearing demons. True, demons are real enough to kill those who believe in them, but the person whose life is hid with Christ in God has been lifted into another sphere of reality where demons have no practical reality. After admitting that there are many gods and many demons, Paul asserts without any reservation, "Yet for us there is one God, the Father, from whom are all things and for whom we exist, and one Lord, Jesus Christ, through whom are all things and through whom we exist" (1 Corinthians 8:6). "For I am sure that neither death, nor life, nor angels, nor principalities, nor things present, nor things to come, nor powers, nor height, nor depth, nor anything else in all creation, will be able to separate us from the love of God in Christ Jesus our Lord" (Romans 8:38, 39).

The prophets, the psalmist, the Mosaic writers, and the apostles are my model. They concentrated on the one all-powerful God who ruled all that was. These pioneers of the faith looked for natural causes for the much feared demons of their pagan neighbors. Thus the Egyptians might fear hail, or river frogs, or lice as demons, but God's people referred to them only as "plagues," and saw them as effects of bad ecology or natural forces. It was seen as horrible apostasy when at times Israel lapsed into the fear of animism and did

obeisance to idols, or sacrificed their daughters and sons
to demons (Psalm 106:37). Likewise it is apostasy for me
to attribute too much power to demons and to fear them.

The Arabs feared bad genies, sprites, demons of the
desolate places, and the hairy ones. But God's prophet
was more likely to translate *lilith* as "hyenas" (Isaiah
13:21, 22). The "night hag" (Isaiah 34:14) was a demon
feared by many people among Israel's neighbors, but Israel's monotheism helped her to live in almost un-
believable freedom from superstition. With Israel's worship concentrated in central sanctuaries its leaders could
watch against inroads of exorcism and cultic practices.
They sternly warned against the occult.

The Prophet Habakkuk was able to debunk and
demythologize the demons most feared by the nations
round about, and the forces the Hebrews themselves
were least able to understand or explain (Habakkuk 3:5,
6). These forces were plague and pestilence, the *resheph*
demons of all the neighbors. Although Habakkuk could
not trace the medical causes of recurring plagues of his
time, he could and did picture them as mere attendants
upon Jehovah when he took to the warpath. They were
like little bodyguards, footmen who ran obediently
ahead of God's chariot and followed behind it! I need
that same exalted view of God's sovereignty and His
triumph over the worst evil powers of my own time.

While Israel's neighbors were busily engaging exorcists and witch doctors to protect them from hail and
thunderbolts, God's people were chanting His praises in
worship psalms, "He gave over their [the Egyptians] cat-
tle to the hail, and their flocks to thunderbolts" (Psalm
78:48).

The persistent demythologizing of the demons of the animists around them occurred times without number and on the part of practically all of God's prophets. They even resorted to gentle, sad satire. Job referred to the feared spirits of the air as sparks that fly upward (Job 5:7). God's people could be serenely safe from the midday sunstroke demon by hiding under Jehovah's wings (Psalm 91:4). The "fiery darts" shot by the Greek god-demon Apollo, "the arrow that flies by day," caused no fear for the person who saw the Lord as "my refuge and my fortress; my God, in whom I trust." (See Psalm 91:1-6.)

The devout Hebrew was aware that a terror he allowed to live and grow within him, subjectively, could seem to become an objective thing that leaped back upon him, seized him, and gripped him (Exodus 15:14, Job 21:6). People in all cultures included some of this in their language. They spoke not only of feeling love or awe, but of being awestruck, or smitten with love. The terror and anguish an about-to-be murdered King Saul felt would have been called a demon by all the animist nations, but God's people called it "cramps" or "anguish" (2 Samuel 1:9).[3]

Persian dualism, which deeply influenced the Jews during the intertestamental period, saw good and bad superpowers, gods of light and darkness, as almost evenly balanced in cosmic struggle. Brought over into the Christian framework, many believers were tempted to see Satan, the tempter, as a sovereign almost equal with God, a being almost as personal as God, a commander of a rival kingdom with cunning almost equal to Almighty God's omniscience.

But in the book which leads our Holy Scriptures the very first time the devil was mentioned at all, he was reduced to a mere "beast," a "wild creature," although a very "subtle" one (Genesis 3:1). How astounding!

Some day I hope my faith can soar to the sublime monotheism of the writer of Genesis 3:1, so that alongside God, Satan is merely a "wild creature." Someday I hope to be able to grant him only this respect even in visceral reaction, in spite of all the terrifying things I know and have seen that Satan can do. I have not yet achieved the grand monotheism of the Bible writers, but I long to achieve it more fully.

As I achieve more and more of such faith, I hope I do not lose my compassion toward animism, toward those who live in fear of evil spirits, and toward deliverance ministers who seek to discern and cast demons out of one another. I personally witnessed a few exorcisms in Africa, such as John Middleton describes in his book listed at the end of this chapter, and I felt deep sadness.

During my time of service in East Africa I worked closely with church leaders within a number of the same tribes in which anthropological studies of sorcery and witchcraft had been made, as reported by Middleton and Winter. I saw them confessing to one another and exhorting one another regarding the new and Christian way to triumph over the world of the spirits.

For Additional Reading and Reference:
Basham, Don. *A Manual for Spiritual Warfare* (Greensburg, Pa.: Manna Books, 1974).
Blatty, William Peter. *The Exorcist* (New York: Bantam Books, 1974).

Davies, T. W. *Magic, Divination, and Demonology Among the Hebrews and Their Neighbors* (New York: Ktav Publishing Co., 1969).

Dawson, George. *Healing: Pagan and Christian* (London: SPCK, 1935).

Enz, Jacob. *The Christian and Warfare* (Scottdale, Pa.: Herald Press, 1972).

Ernst, Victor H. *I Talked with Spirits* (Wheaton: Tyndale, 1970).

Freed, Stanley and Ruth. *Magic, Witchcraft, and Curing* (New York: Natural History Press, 1967).

Gasson, Raphael. *The Challenging Counterfeit: A Former Medium Exposes Spiritualism* (Plainfield, N.J.: Logos, 1966, 1972).

Henderson, Glenna. *My Name Is Legion* (Minneapolis: Bethany Fellowship, 1972).

Middleton, John, and Winter, S. H. *Witchcraft and Sorcery in East Africa* (New York: Frederick and Praeger, 1964).

Peterson, William J. *Those Curious New Cults* (New Canaan, Conn.: Keats, 1973).

Vogt, E. Z., and Lessa, William. *A Reader in Comparative Religion* (New York: Harpers, 1965).

7
God Asks Me to Look for Natural Causes, Too

Christians view their sovereign God as one who rules partly through reliable laws of nature. Sequences of cause and effect are predictable. This is the foundation rock of science, and of the laws of health and of medicine.

Whereas leprosy used to be the most "demonic" of all sicknesses for both missionary and animist, God chose to provide relief for leprosy not through exorcisms but through medicine. God created herbs for the service of mankind. God gave humanity the wisdom to develop preventative and curative medicine. Even though leprosy was seen as a type of sin, curable only by a startling miracle, God's quiet miracle of medical advance proved most helpful. Just as God sends His gracious rain upon both the evil and the good, so He gives His quiet miracles to medical researchers who are Christians and to those who are not.

Just as the Mosaic writers insisted on reducing Egypt's demons of thunderbolt and hail to mere "plagues," so Christians should be helping to reduce the demonized areas of fear and suffering to some of their natural causes—to causes persons can begin to do something about through the patient dedication of loving service, suffering love, medical care, and pastoral counseling. The Roman Catholic Church has forbidden any bishop to authorize an exorcism service (to solve a person's problem by naming and casting out a demon) unless a fresh medical examination and a fresh psychiatric examination have first been conducted. It is precisely at this point that many, if not most, Protestant exorcists whom I know and have read about are most remiss. Very few show this same respect for God's gifts through medicine and this same humility about their own readiness and ability to diagnose.

Even though demon-idols, fear of evil spirits, and exorcism rituals to give protection from vengeful gods were very much a part of the lives of all of their neighbors, the Mosaic writers mentioned only once "the gods of Egypt." The prophets kept looking much closer for the cause of their troubles. They kept pointing to the pride and disobedience of the hearts of God's own people. They decried the injustices to the poor, the arrogance of their kings, and the loss of a sense of being the covenant people of God.

The Gospel writers, Matthew and Luke, as they retold Mark's miracle-exorcism stories tended to introduce more natural causes. Exorcisms began to be lumped together with other healings. Compare the way Mark 1:39 is described in Matthew 4:23, and the way Mark 3:9-11 is retold in Luke 6:17-19. Infirmity, dumbness, blindness, epilepsy, and insanity all tended to become sickness, requiring "healing."

The last of the Gospel writers, John, included no

exorcism stories at all and never associated infirmity, blindness, or deafness with demon possession as Mark had done. John linked demon possession rather with the life of Judas, and traced it to the "natural cause" of his known sin, his covered up stealing of money (John 12:6), and his anger (instead of repentance) when he was exposed by Jesus (John 13:27-30). Because of these down-to-earth natural causes, "the devil entered into Judas." It follows that, if Judas were to be helped, he would need to have been confronted at these same natural causes of selfishness, stealing, anger, and pride which led him into sin.

It is not necessary or helpful to say when I surrender to sin, "The devil made me do it." My human selfishness coupled with human freedom is enough. I was created with the image of God, a little lower than the angels, the psalmist says, but crowned with such glory and honor that I can be set over God's creation as co-regent. I can also choose to align myself with all the prodigal powers and persons grouped against God Almighty.

If I misuse my freedom, and choose selfishly to defy God, and combine my tremendous powers with those of other rebel human beings, there is no need to look farther, to blame the devil, for the tragic results. The demon that tempted Balaam, in Numbers 21, was his hunger for power. That is often my demon as well!

When I choose to obey Satan, the prince of the power of the air, it is a rebound from my first and prior choice to disobey God. It is the result of a "natural cause," in that I chose to walk in the appetites and lusts of the flesh.

It is a cop out, Paul told the Ephesian congregation,

to blame their sin on the devil, because they were merely choosing to fulfill the desires of the flesh and the mind (Ephesians 2:2, 3). Every basic desire of a person is good and right, if utilized, expressed, released, and satisfied within the life of covenant love with God and neighbor and family as God intended. The problem comes when my natural desires are satisfied selfishly, outside of God's perfect will for my happiness.

Rather than building up an eerie dread and a superstitious fear of discarnate spirits, demons who flit about trying to get into the body, the epistles everywhere discuss the "natural causes" and preventative measures. Lest I should give place to the devil I am to watch out for the natural cause—going to bed angry or letting the sun go down on my wrath (Ephesians 4:26).

Lest Satan tempt a marriage partner through lack of self-control, Paul warns in 1 Corinthians 7:5 to be considerate of one another's sex needs. Don't get outsmarted by Satan, he warns again in 2 Corinthians 2:5-11. Be quick to forgive and to comfort someone who has failed and is repentant, and show that you still love him very much. The natural cause of trouble is the discouragement, disappointment, and despair of the repentant person who needs love so very badly.

Look carefully at the "natural causes" which lay behind Eve's yielding to Satan in the Garden of Eden. Notice her natural desire to be smart, her desire for fun, and for pleasure. Notice her natural tendency to be suspicious, to resent limits or restraints. Consider her natural longings for immediate physical gratification, contrasted with her problem in giving priority to her fellowship with her Maker. Observe her natural rivalry with Adam, her husband, and their all-too-common tendency to want to be one-up on each other. Notice her problem believing that God's perfect love does withhold some things sometimes.

Behind the messenger of Satan sent to buffet Paul he saw a natural cause, a thorn in the flesh. Think how much pain he endured. Think of his frustrated hopes for healing, of the limits his thorn in the flesh imposed upon his relationship with other people, of the way his work program likely had to be curtailed. Think of his humiliation because he who had helped heal so many others could not receive healing himself. All of these "natural causes" likely made up his problem.

At a three-day seminar called to study exorcism I ate lunch with three psychiatrists, all of whom had served many demonized patients. They had seen all of the "signs" which exorcists insist are the sure proofs of possession. They accepted the reality of the devil and were reverent, active, evangelical Christians. But they agreed that all of these signs are also identifiable medically and psychiatrically. All the signs are traceable to natural causes. As concerned medical and psychiatric specialists they were committed to keep on working at the natural causes.

The Christian should not be too ready to assign demonic causes to phenomena of parapsychology and psychic manifestations that are difficult to understand. Christians should continue the noble tradition of the Old Testament prophets in this regard. I have continued to read, with mild interest, the validated research findings from parapsychology research centers—from J. B. Rhine's early book, *The Reach of the Mind,* to Martin

Ebon's recent *The Devil's Bride.* But because I do not understand certain powers of the mind does not mean that I must call these things demonic.

Why not allow a merely human area of marvel, because man is so fearfully and wonderfully made? Why insist, as so many Protestant exorcists do, that hypnotism is of the devil? Why see something sinister in water dousing or water witching? Why assign the most fearsome meanings to wart removals, levitation (objects appearing to float in midair), pendulums, and the like which some ethnic groups carry on?

Why insist that the use of drugs is totally bad when taken without prescription, and totally good when prescribed by a medical doctor? It seems to me that the same activity, hypnosis for instance, may be a good, honorable, and helpful activity if carried on with the right motives, and wrong if done as black magic.

Obviously, I must studiously avoid dabbling in any activity with those who seek to worship the devil. I must refuse to participate in even the most innocent activity if the group is deliberately moving in defiance of the God of Hebrew Christian revelation, or of God's Son, Jesus Christ. I take seriously the Apostle Paul's warning, "You cannot drink the cup of the Lord and the cup of demons" (1 Corinthians 10:21).

My own attitude is, hopefully, like that of the Apostle Paul stated in 1 Timothy 4:4, 5, "For everything created by God is good, and nothing is to be rejected if it is received with thanksgiving; for then it is consecrated by the word of God and prayer." I welcome discoveries into the reaches of the mind and the previously uncharted potentials of the human spirit because man is fearfully and wonderfully made.

Paul called it a "doctrine of demons" when people taught avoidance of God's good gifts, like the eating of certain foods, or the enjoyment of sex within marriage. He called it "giving heed to deceitful spirits" merely to create a taboo against marriage or against a certain food (1 Timothy 4:1-3). As a convinced monotheist, I believe I should take a basically positive attitude toward God's world, toward God's gifts of food, sex, mind, emotion, extrasensory perception, and most of the vast and mysterious powers of the human mind. They are merely human and can be utilized for good or evil.

As to astrology, I tend to agree with Augustine that the Magi were the last ones who were divinely guided by the stars. Since Christ appeared, God's Word to us is, "This is my beloved Son, hear Him."

Astrology may be fairly innocent on the surface. But it seems to have a vortex effect. Astrology diverts man's quest from the living God of Hebrew-Christian revelation and sucks him into the vortex of the occult, the weird, the magical, and the religious underworld. The apostasy of Manassah described in 2 Chronicles 33 appears to be an example of this.

Personally, I like the attitude of Jeremiah. He referred to the whole demonic realm as "worthlessness" or "vanity" (Jeremiah 2:5). Alongside the power of the omnipotent Jehovah he knew so well and trusted so completely, all the rest was lacking in substance and ultimate reality. Jeremiah warned God's people that if they gave much attention to demons they too would become "feeble ones" like the demon-gods of Babylonia and Assyria.

I like Gamaliel's attitude too when he said, "If this is of God don't fight it, and if it's not it will come to nothing." So don't sweat it.

Some astronomer-astrologers tell us that Aries the Ram dominated the heavens from 2000 BC to 0, the period of God the Father. Then Pisces the fish was the controlling influence for the next 2,000-year era of God the Son. Now, they say, we are entering the Aquarian age of God the Holy Spirit which will last until AD 4000. How interesting! If the Aquarian age is to be one of shedding of inhibitions, of new spiritual adventures, of ecstasies, of joy, of amity, and of aspirations, that's fine with me! I'll keep a sense of humor toward the whole astrology business, but look elsewhere for my guidance.

I intend to keep open to extrasensory perception as God gives it through his charismatic word-of-knowledge. I have known and cherished a "Spirit-driven word of consensus" in a group engaged in prayerful search for God's leading. I will be slow to criticize the interpreted tongues of charismatic groups, even though many I have heard have turned out to be so trite as to be almost meaningless.

I intend to walk humbly with my God, believing that my life is in His hand, that He intervenes and leads in many ways, that there is mystery and miracle even in the most commonplace. I intend to keep on praying to God for help, for guidance in large and small decisions, and for healing if I am sick.

I am prepared to regard as "human" a lot of trance speaking, apparitions, automatic writing, precognition, photography of auras around the head of certain per-

sons, sleepwalking, card laying, planting vegetables by
the sign of the moon, premonition in dreams, color
therapy, respect for relics from beloved ancestors,
chimney noises in haunted houses, chain letters, finding
four-leaf clovers, telepathic communication between
loved ones, transference, tongues speaking, hex signs,
powwow rituals which rely upon human suggestibility,
and conversing with plants. I am glad that men of
science have banded together in a Spiritual Frontiers
Fellowship to study and experiment in parapsychology
and to find some of the natural causes which lie behind
these and other strange phenomena.

Early anthropology researchers felt that the advance
of medical services would end the "savage" notion that
spirits roam about looking for a host, an animal or
person in which to be embodied. But recent studies like
Martin Ebon's *The Devil's Bride* or John Richards' *But
Deliver Us from Evil,* reveal that the invading spirits have
merely changed names. If a spiritually alert and im-
aginative neighbor reported hordes of little black
demons whizzing around in her head, I'd try to secure
for her a thorough medical examination, expecting that
likely these "spots before her eyes" might be eased by
suitable doses of liver extract and vitamin B_{12}. I would
agree with Richards (p. 105) that "our Lord would be
well pleased" with such a healing.

I cannot in all good conscience label epilepsy as demonic, or asthma, schizophrenia, hysteria, conversion
hysteria, cancer, or leukemia. I cannot call them a disease
in one friend or neighbor and a demon in another.

I cannot label the well-documented cases of animal
possession (Richards, p. 148) as demon possession.

Neither unusual strength nor unusual knowledge are proofs, in themselves, that a person is possessed. Catatonic falling, changes of voice, foaming at the mouth, ability to predict, speaking in tongues, changes in demeanor or appearance all have natural causes, too, which can be diagnosed by competent medical doctors and psychiatrists.

For any person showing the above symptoms I would try to secure the best in medical and psychiatric care, the warmest in forgiving and loving milieu, and the strongest in intercessory prayer support. These are the best avenues of relief I know for such sufferers.

During a recent illness of a dear friend, my prayers for his healing continued and intensified while he underwent more and more specialized medical tests to find out the "natural causes" of his baffling illness. I prayed for God's power to move through the doctor's diagnosis and treatment or to heal in ways no one could understand, whichever way God willed. My friend was at a highly specialized center where the best of blood studies, brain scans, muscular biopsies, myelograms, and X-rays were all available. But this did not lessen my reliance upon God's mysterious answers to prayer. In my world-view, prayer and medical care are both normal ways God works. I do not let up on the one to trust the other.

I have dealt with many "Dr. Jekyl and Mr. Hyde" types during my experiences as chaplain in mental hospitals. But I do not believe that every split personality is demonized. Many cases of split personality are documented in psychiatric records.

Flora R.Schreiber in her book *Sybil* reports portions

of nine years of therapy with a woman whose personality was splintered into sixteen distinct and separate identities. The poor woman operated coherently and consistently for periods of time in one of her persons and under that person's name. Then she experienced some "forgotten days" during which she shifted over to another distinct "person and name" within herself.

Sybil is probably the most detailed record of the therapy of a split personality which has ever been published. The words "demon," or "devil," or "exorcism" do not appear in the index of the 424-page book. I am not uncomfortable that the therapist does not identify a demon within this devout but troubled woman. I am satisfied that the therapist looked for "natural causes" and that the badly splintered personality was healed. All healing is God's gift, and I want to give Him the thanks and praise for it all.

For Additional Reading and Reference:
Collins, Gary R. *The Christian Psychology of Paul Tournier* (Grand Rapids: Baker, 1973).

Mallory, James D. *The Kink and I* (Grand Rapids: Victor Books, 1974).

McCasland, Vernon. *By the Finger of God* (New York: Mcmillan, 1951).

Oates, Wayne E. *When Religion Gets Sick* (Philadelphia: Westminster Press, 1970).

Peterson, Robert. *Are Demons for Real?* (Chicago: Moody Press, 1972).

Schreiber, Flora R. *Sybil* (Chicago: Henry Regnery, 1973).

Skrade, Carol. *God and the Grotesque* (Philadelphia:

Westminster Press, 1974).

Smith, Nancy C. *Journey Out of Nowhere* (Waco: Word, 1973).

Wright, J. Stafford. *Christianity and the Occult* (Chicago: Moody Press, 1972).

——————————. *Mind, Man, and the Spirits* (Grand Rapids: Zondervan, 1972).

8
God's Son Defeated the Devil Decisively

I find it inspiring to study the life and work of Jesus as *Christus Victor*, Christ the Victor. His victory over the devil was as definitive and irreversible as God's creation of the worlds, or as the final consummation.

Jesus saw His ministry as an enlargement of the work of Moses. Just as Moses had led disorganized slaves out of their demon-laden environment in Egypt, so Jesus would lead God's people, enslaved again to demons, to a new and better victory. God called Jesus to the Mount of Transfiguration to discuss, along with Moses, the "new Exodus" Jesus would accomplish in Jerusalem. During their years of captivity in Babylon, and the years without a powerful prophet among them, Israel had picked up superstitions again, demon fears, and exorcism rituals, until they were about as confused as when Moses led Israel from Egyptian demonism.

The exorcists of Egypt used their rituals to try to match the miracles of Moses. They could, by exorcism rituals, duplicate the first three miracles of Moses—turn rods into serpents, change the Nile water into blood, and cause the Nile to swarm with frogs. But when Moses struck the dust of the earth and turned it to gnats, they could not duplicate the feat through their secret arts. They gave up in awed consternation! They announced to the king that a new power had superseded theirs. They cried, "This is the finger of God!" (Exodus 8:19). Moses proceeded to give new laws, new victory, and new power for the life of God's new people, freed from bondage, freed from fear of demons, free to serve their sovereign King.

Just as demon fears and exorcistic cures faded out among the Jews soon after the victory of Moses in Exodus, No. 1, so the sublime victory Jesus wrought over the devil caused exorcism to fade out in the new people, the church, created by Christ's Spirit. Exorcisms, so stark and prominent in the Book of Mark, were generalized and classified along with other illnesses in the records by Matthew and Luke, and were dropped from the "good news" altogether by the time the writer of the Gospel of John came along.

Jesus viewed His life, death, resurrection, and church-forming as one mighty, cosmic victory. The entire Christ event was the seed of the woman crushing the serpent's head. It was the stronger one binding the weaker. The prince of this world was cast out.

Jesus claimed by faith the Father's Word that His death on Calvary would cast out the ruler of this world (John 12:31). Calvary's victory was the final exorcism, the cosmic one, the decisive event which forever reset the nature of the conflict with demonic powers. The Apostle Paul came to the same conclusion as he declared to the congregation at Colossae, "He disarmed the principalities and powers and made a public example of them, triumphing over them in [the cross]" (Colossians 2:15). Calvary's victory left the principalities and powers depleted, drained of power, defeated, held up to derision, and diminished.

Christ refused to use the all-too-common deliverance rituals of the other religious experts. In contrast to Hellenistic exorcistic rituals, he used no formula of, "I adjure you by . . .," and no charms. He did not heal during dreams or draw out vivid details of the illness. He took no money for His services. He never touched the genitals, mocked the demons, or used entrails of animals. He never exorcized demons to help women conceive. His use of saliva in healing was one of the very few times he allowed His methods to coincide with those of pagan exorcists.

Christ refused also the patterns used by Jewish exorcists. He used no gibberish or speaking in tongues as part of His ritual. He used no roots, plants, or magic rings. He drew out no lists of sins. He never adjured "by the bones of Solomon"—an earlier exorcist much quoted by rabbinic exorcists. He used no imprecatory prayers, scolding, or cursing of the demon. Jesus called up no benign ancestral spirits to help do battle with evil ancestral spirits. He did not "blow the demons away" by breathing on them, as some exorcists did.[1]

Jesus cast out demons "by the finger of God," as a sign that Exodus, No. 2, was happening. He stressed the inauguration of a new phase of the kingdom of God. He did it as one more way to help people believe. He was careful not to evoke lists of sins or to allow the impression that the feeble folk, the woman with an infirmity, the epileptic, the groping blind man, the paralytics, the miserable child falling into the fire, and the deaf mute were somehow the worst sinners in Israel. To Jesus it was the evil principalities and powers, the corrupt but outwardly correct religious leaders who were "of your father, the devil."

Jesus seemed most concerned that the deeper and profounder significance of His exorcisms be clear. He commanded the demons to be silent, and told the healed demonic to report the event as God having mercy on him. Jesus stressed the meaning behind the mere incidents.

In Mark's narratives the incidents are used primarily to drive home the larger truth of Christ's divine authority (Mark 1:23-28), and the spreading fame of Jesus in Galilee. Nothing at all is said about the later life of the healed person. Although the early church soon added fasting to their ritual of exorcism, Christ used it little, if at all.[2]

In the incident of the Gadarene demonic, Jesus was preparing for His crucial teaching against the scribes and Pharisees in Mark 7:1-23. He was determined to combat their elaborate legalism regarding who and what was clean or unclean. So He ministered to the unclean Gentiles, the Gerasenes or Gadarenes (Mark 5:1) near the unclean tomb (verse 2) and met a man with an unclean spirit. He sent the unclean spirits into the unclean swine (verse 13). They wanted to stay in an unclean or haunted region. But Christ came to cleanse the unclean and to put a stop to Pharisee avoidance.

Soon afterward an unclean woman, with an issue of unclean blood, touched Him and was healed (Mark 5:34). He told the disciples how to shake off the unclean dust from their feet and to hallow a new house church with their salutation of blessing and benediction.

Mark stressed Christ rescuing outcasts from the unclean category into which the Jews had consigned them. He reported Christ's work in unclean Tyre and Sidon, casting a spirit out of the daughter of an unclean Greek, a Syrophoenician woman (Mark 7:24-30). He went on to feed the unclean crowd of 4,000 as recorded in Mark 8:1-10.

Mark used the next exorcism story, the poor deaf-mute lad of Mark 9:14-29, to drive home the fact that prayer—not exorcistic ritual—was the most effective and powerful way to help such persons. When the disciples came privately to ask why they failed, He called them a "faithless generation," and chided them for lack of prayer (Luke 9:19 and 29).

The disciples, who later became the apostles of the newly founded church, never forgot Christ's teachings. Christ had taught them that united prayer, focused lovingly upon the head of the distressed person, is to replace the exorcistic demon expelling rituals so prevalent in other religions. Let the other religions of the world go on with their exorcisms. But Christ, as Moses had done, was shaping another way of victory.

The disciples noticed too that Christ never identified a demon in any of them, addressed their demon, nor cast one from them. When Peter failed, Jesus still addressed Peter and called him to repent. Even though He said, "Get thee behind me Satan," Jesus was holding Peter responsible.

Even when Jesus knew that Judas was yielding to his love of money and to his disappointments with Jesus, and that Satan was entering Judas, Jesus still addressed

Judas and never his demon. He called Judas himself to repent. Christ seldom used exorcism in Judea itself, but only in pagan fringe areas like Galilee, as part of His outreach evangelism.

When the disciples recounted some successes as exorcists (as many modern deliverance ministers love to do), Christ rebuked them for it. He told them to rejoice rather in God's grace, that they belong to Christ, and that their names are written in heaven.

When Jesus announced what it was that He felt most called to do, because the Spirit of Jehovah was on Him, He conspicuously omitted exorcism. He felt called to give sight to blind and to preach jubilee year of social leveling (Luke 4:16-21). He echoed His mother's lullaby, "He has filled the hungry with good things, and the rich he has sent empty away" (Luke 1:53).

When Christ told John's messengers what He was actually doing, to revive the faith of imprisoned John that He was really the Messiah, He omitted mention of His exorcisms. When the Apostle John cited seven miracle-signs of Christ's deity, he conspicuously omitted the exorcism miracles Christ had done. I believe that these down-playings of exorcisms were conscious, deliberate, and intended to further a trend.

Christ refused to allow exorcism, the naming and casting out of demons, to become a mark of the new movement He was beginning. When He reminded questioners that, "Your sons cast out devils," He was referring to Jews who likely did not believe in Him at all. Jesus did give His disciples the authority to cast out demons, so they too could cope with confrontations they might experience. But He carefully avoided allow-

ing exorcism to become a major concern of His future
church.

Christ insisted that the church He would found would
not stress exorcism. He warned that some exorcists
would imagine that this exploit was somehow a mark of
His movement, a sign of His power, a proof that they
were Christ's servants. But He warned that He might
need to tell exorcists who cast out devils in his name, "I
never knew you; depart from me, you evildoers" (Matthew 7:23).

Two times Christ used the Greek word *ekklesia,*
which is translated "church." Both times, as He outlined
what would be the central emphasis of His church, He
omitted mentioning exorcism altogether. In Matthew
16:18 He implied that where the confessing person is
sharing the newest revelation which Father in heaven is
giving about who Jesus really is, precisely then Jesus will
be building His church.

In Matthew 18:17 He saw the church as a reconciling
fellowship in which persons dare to confront and forgive
one another honestly. Amidst all the mention of binding
and loosing and forgiving sin, there is no hint that exorcism might have a place.

What seemed to be the natural causes of demonism as
seen in Mark? The demonic as reported in Mark was
often a person who was ambivalent about his commitment. Mark 1:21-27 showed a Jew in a synagogue who
flatly rejected Jesus, being forced to admit that Jesus
was after all the Holy One of God! Synagogues full of
ambivalence and rejection were the scene of many such
exorcisms (Mark 1:39). Christ silenced the testimonies
of these ambivalent persons (Mark 1:34).

Demonic activity was suspected by some Jews wherever there was great strength or intense activity, as when they said of Christ Himself, "He is possessed by Beelzebul" (Mark 3:22). But Christ knew that fervency, focused around a clear sense of call and vocation, was not demonic. He saw the demonic in the double-minded person, and not in the agitated individual.

Neither the presence of sin in a person, nor even the presence of debiliting sickness and sin, dared always be construed as caused by a demon. Christ healed and forgave the paralytic (Mark 2:1-12). He seemed to prefer to heal and forgive without exorcism. He did it this way with the man with the withered hand (Mark 3:1-6), but when exorcism erupted he urged silence about it and left the area (Mark 3:7-12).

Christ wanted people to avoid the spookish, ethereal notions of demonism so prevalent at the time, and to locate demonism more simply in an ambivalent attitude toward Him (Mark 1:24); in a divided loyalty (Mark 3:26); in an inattentive listening to the Word (Mark 4:15, 16); in the dramatic swing from the desire for all prayer on the Mount of Transfiguration to no prayer at all while helping the boy in the valley (Mark 9:14-29); and in defiant swine-keeping by rebellious Jews, sneering at their upbringing (Mark 5:1-20).

He did not point out a demon in the stormy wind, as their folklore might have suggested. But He did identify the demonic in the ambivalence of the Jewish pig keepers of Gadara who banished a deviant to the graveyard (Mark 5:1-20).

He saw nothing demonic in the sickness of Jairus' daughter, or the woman with the issue of blood.

Although Christ taught His disciples explicitly how to pray, He obviously did not give His disciples an exorcism ritual to use, whereby they would take command in Christ's name and order devils to depart. Theirs was a preaching ministry, with a call to decisive repentance, and anointing with oil (Mark 6:13). The authority to perform exorcisms was likely an interim thing, to be used until His Spirit founded the church.

Christ seemed to try to avoid forming a standard healing ritual. He allowed many to be healed by merely touching the hem of His garment, and saw nothing demonic in their plight (Mark 6:56). When the Syrophoenician woman insisted on calling her daughter's plight demon possession, He healed the child without an exorcism, in absentia (Mark 7:24-30). He saw nothing demonic in the deaf and dumb person of Decapolis (Mark 7:31-37), nor in the blind man of Bethsaida (Mark 8:22-26), nor in blind Bartimaeus (Mark 10:46-52).

Christ quickly pointed out the demonic, however, in Peter's attempt to rebuke Him for His intended suffering (Mark 8:33), and in the boy's anguish before disciples powerless from lack of prayer (Mark 9:14-29). The demon to be cast out was indecision, ambivalence, dishonesty, or deceit about commitment to Christ.

Christ several times warned against the practice of naming a demon in another person. He knew what this felt like! Some doubtlessly sincere Jews told Him to His face, "You have a devil." He knew the implied insult. He felt the insinuation that, "You no longer are responsible." He saw it as a form of name calling, as stereotyping, and as very demeaning.

He deeply resented the all-too-common tendency to

identify as a demon in someone else a trait or charac-
teristic which was currently unpopular. Many Jews dis-
liked Samaritans, so they identified a "Samaritan devil"
in anyone they did not like! Jesus implied a stern warning against naming as a demon in someone else what
actually may turn out to be a working of God's Spirit
within him. After His own inner Spirit was identified as
the demon Beelzebul, Christ called such demon naming
the unpardonable sin, a blasphemy of God's Holy Spirit
(Mark 3:22-30).

For me, this warning by Christ is so serious that I
could never presume to name a demon in a disturbed
person. I might be guilty of blasphemy! I might lay an
extra burden of unworthiness upon an already burdened
soul.

I believe that Jesus knew that His death and resurrection was the basic, cosmic exorcism and victory over the
devil. He dared to believe that His Spirit would create a
new people, bringing their whole lives into His way of
life, so that exorcism would have no more place in
Christ's church than it had in Israel before the captivity.
Every smaller, individual exorcism Christ performed
was a metaphor, a sign pointing to the final, full,
supreme, cosmic exorcism Christ would perform by His
teaching, death, resurrection, and forming of a fellowship by His outpoured Holy Spirit.

I am well aware that some deliverance ministers claim
that the mere name of Jesus forces demons to name
themselves. I can only say that I do not find this to be
true either in Christ's own life, nor in the most of the
preachings recorded in the New Testament, nor in the
majority of the preachings of missionary history.

For Additional Reading and Reference:
Eitren, S. *Some Notes on the Demonology in the New Testament* (Oslave: Typis Espressit, 1950).
Erdman, Charles. *Remember Jesus Christ* (Grand Rapids: Eerdmans, 1958).
Harper, Michael. *Spiritual Warfare: Defeating Satan in the Christian Life* (Plainfield, N.J.: Logos, 1970).
Hunter, Archibald M. *Interpreting the Parables* (Philadelphia: Westminster Press, 1961).
Lundström, Gösta. *The Kingdom of God in the Teaching of Jesus* (Richmond, Va.: John Knox, 1963).
Manson, William. *The Way of the Cross* (Richmond, Va.: John Knox, 1958).
McCasland, Vernon. *The Pioneer of Our Faith—A New Life of Jesus* (New York: McGraw Hill, 1964).
Moule, C.F.D. *Colossians and Philemon* (New York: Cambridge University Press, 1968).
Richardson, Carl. *Exorcism: New Testament Style* (Old Tappan, N.J.: Revell, 1974).

9
I Can Defeat Satan
Through Repentance and Faith

The apostles apparently accepted Christ's exorcisms as one proof of Christ's deity, along with those miracles which John specifically cites as "signs." These include walking on the water, raising Lazarus from the dead, stilling the storm, changing the water into wine, and such astounding miracles.

But in the churches they addressed in the epistles, the apostles did not urge the use of exorcism rites to cast out demons (because Christ had done such miracles) any more than they urged stilling storms or turning water into wine. In the letters to young churches, the apostles never mention Christ's exorcisms. Much less do they encourage the young churches to imitate Jesus as an exorcist.

Every time the apostles mention Satan and his wiles, they either assume or say explicitly that active repentance and faith is the way of victory. Always they seem to assume that a lust of the flesh can be identified as the source of the trouble. Always they hold the person responsible to believe in God's saving power, to repent, and to turn to God in an act of faith.

One exception to the general avoidance of exorcism on the part of the apostles in their letters to young churches is Paul's exorcism of an evil spirit from the slave girl at Philippi (Acts 16:18). This was indeed a genuine case of exorcism in the classic model.

But the fortune-telling slave girl was not a member of the congregation at Philippi. Although he used exorcism outside the church, Paul did not recommend it for Euodia and Syntyche who were causing trouble inside the congregation (Philippians 4:2).

Paul avoided exorcism of the fortune-teller as long as he could. He resorted to exorcism only after the fortune-teller had harassed him for several days. He ignored the incident when he wrote to the congregation at Philippi.

In fact, although ten persons troublesome to the Apostle Paul have been named in the congregations Paul served, he never cast a devil from any of them. It was simply not Paul's way to help a Christian to victory over Satan.

The writings of many present-day exorcists and deliverance ministers cite blasphemy as one of the marks of demon possession which calls for exorcism. Blasphemy indicates to them that a person is overpowered by the evil one, possessed by him, so that he cannot take responsibility for his own life and decide to repent. But in dealing with two blasphemers, Hymenaeus and Alexander, Paul held them personally responsible. He excommunicated them, as persons, from the church. He called this "delivering them to Satan," a forceful call to repent. Paul held them accountable for their behavior. He represented reality to them, insisting that they be placed outside the church where their self-chosen loyalties already were (1 Timothy 1:18-20). Not exorcism, but excommunication was Paul's way to encourage them to repent. Paul knew of Christ's exorcisms. He knew that converts from heathenism were accustomed to it and expected it. But refused to resort to exorcism with these men.

None of the apostles ever told of a believer becoming possessed by a demon so that he was helpless and needed to be exorcised. Even though Paul told the sorcerer he was a "son of the devil," he still called upon him to repent (Acts 13:10).

Peter admitted that Satan had filled the heart of Ananias to lie to the Holy Ghost, but Peter still spoke to Ananias and not to his demon. Peter did not perform an exorcism. He held Ananias responsible to the very end (Acts 5:1-6). Peter refused to perform an exorcism even when a life was at stake.

When Peter discerned that Simon, the former sorcerer, was in the bond of iniquity, he still held him responsible to repent. Simon did so and asked for prayer (Acts 8:22 and 24).

John joined the other apostles in calling for personal responsibility, and for a decisive act of repentance and faith, as the only way of victory over the devil. John omitted the alibi that Judas had been bribed to betray Jesus, as the earlier gospel writers had said. John instead emphasized that Judas himself was responsible. He had chosen to be a thief (John 12:6). John shows that Jesus was gently calling Judas to repentance (6:70, 13:27, and 13:30). John reported the dramatic call to repentance when Jesus handed Judas the morsel of food, pointing out just who the betrayer was. Jesus held Judas totally responsible to repent, even though he said that the devil put it into Judas' heart to betray Jesus (John 13:2).

John reported that although the Pharisees were of their father the devil, they themselves were responsible to repent (John 8:44).

According to John, I can not claim that "the devil made me do it" because my environment is so bad. He wrote to believers in Pergamos, "where Satan's throne is," but he insisted that they repent (Revelation 12, 13, 16). John's last appeal to the church at Ephesus, as he saw them losing their first love, was for them to repent (Revelation 2:5).

James insisted that we Christians admit that our temptations do not arise from God's testings. Rather God has begotten us as sons, and desires that we become the first fruits of His redeemed creation. James pointed out that temptations arise from our own inner desires. He insisted that we take ownership of them and full responsibility for them (James 1:12-15). Our undisciplined desires bring forth selfish living, sin, and eventually death.

Both John and James insisted that victory over the seductions of evil, whether arising from inner desires or from evil persons nearby, requires a walking in the light of God. John urged that we walk out into the light as Christ is in the light, inviting the scrutiny of God's all-seeing eyes, and living before one another and the face of God in that light in which no lie can hide. In that forgiving fellowship the blood of Christ goes on cleansing us from sin (1 John 1:7).

James echoed John's urging when he said, "Confess your sins to one another, and pray for one another, that

you may be healed" (James 5:16). John added that giving testimony to one another, and testifying of our faith
to the outside world, is a way to overcome the wicked
one (Revelation 12:11). In a later chapter I will trace in
more detail the way in which the apostles assumed that
honest and vital sharing in a Holy Spirit permeated congregational fellowship is the secret of victory over the
devil, and the strongest resource against his wiles.

Even when John discussed a "sin unto death," so
severe as to seem almost unpardonable, and so far gone
that, "I do not say you should pray for it," there was no
hint that such a drastic case called for an exorcism
(1 John 5:16).

In Romans Paul listed the sins of the pagans, and then
the sins of the Jewish people (Romans 1-3). His assumption always was that the way of repentance, turning
from sin by an act of the will upon conviction by the
Holy Spirit, remained the way of hope for every person.
He listed no category of those who were not capable of
repenting, so that the evangelist must talk to their
demon and not directly to the individual.

To the Ephesian congregation Paul recommended the
quiet miracles, the Holy Spirit power over the long pull,
as the way to overcome the modern exorcists—the Jannes and Jambres who had withstood Moses (referring to
Exodus 7). Paul seemed to avoid the showdown type of
confrontation (2 Timothy 3:8).

Do the apostles avoid exorcism because they see
Satan already defeated? Do the apostles claim Christ's
once-for-all victory over Satan, and think about the demonic as entering into a victory already won? I believe
they do.

In one word picture after another the Christian is urged to regard Satan or the devil as already defeated. Not only in heaven's war has Satan been a loser (Revelation 12:7-9), but his furious period of early activity has been cut short (Revelation 12:12).

The early Christians, in the new victory of resurrection life and Spirit power, crushed him underfoot (Romans 16:20). They saw personalized evil as defeated, disarmed, displayed like a humiliated war prisoner alongside of Christ's victory on His cross (Colossians 2:15). To the extent that they thought about fallen angels at all, it was to reflect upon their helpless bound-in-chains condition (Jude 6).

To them Satan is crushed already, rendered less powerful than the believers (Hebrews 2:14). Jesus Christ's victory has dealt Satan a crushing defeat. Satan's whole falsity has been exposed and judged (John 16:11). His works are destroyed (1 John 3:8). He can only flee when a Christian resists him (James 4:7). A Christian calls him to heel as one would a dog, "Get thee behind me."

Christians exult continuously in their freedom from captivity to evil, because Christ the stronger one has rendered ineffective and powerless the devil, the personalized force of evil (Mark 3:27). The kingship of God, begun when Christ cast out demons, has forever made oppression by personalized evil unnecessary for the believer (Luke 10:18). Christians can overcome evil (Romans 12:21). Believers have turned from the power of Satan to God (Acts 26:18).

Christians are to preach, to discuss joyously, and to claim constantly their deliverance from the kingdom of darkness (Colossians 1:13). Sadly, they observe persons outside the church still being taken captive by Satan at his will (2 Timothy 2:26). By loving teaching which calls sinners to repentance and faith, they set about freeing anyone who wishes to awaken and turn to the truth. They do not need to brood fearfully about the devil. Barely mentioning him, they concentrate upon exalting Jesus Christ, because "he who is in you is greater than he who is in the world" (1 John 4:4).

For Additional Reading and Reference:

Basham, Don. *True and False Prophets* (Greensburg, Pa.: Manna Books, 1973).

Christenson, Larry. *A Message to the Charismatic Movement* (Minneapolis: Dimension Books, 1972).

Dodds, C. H., *The Apostolic Preaching and Its Development* (New York: Willett Clark and Co., 1937).

Glen, Stanley. *The Recovery of the Teaching Ministry* (Philadelphia: Westminster Press, 1960).

Mackintosh, H. R. *The Christian Experience of Forgiveness* (New York: Collins, 1961).

Miller, Donald G. *Conqueror in Chains* (Philadelphia: Westminster Press, 1951).

Miller, William A. *Why Do Christians Break Down?* (Minneapolis: Augsburg, 1973).

Weatherspoon, J. B. *Sent Forth to Preach* (New York: Harper and Bros., 1954).

10
Mutual Prayer and
Teaching Lead to Victory

When Satan desired to have Peter that he might "sift him as wheat," Jesus demonstrated what He constantly taught, that intercessory prayer is the most effective way to help a fellow Christian undergoing test. "I have prayed for you that your faith may not fail" (Luke 22:32).

Instead of individually casting demons out of one another, Christ taught that Christians should pray "the deliverance prayer" for one another. Encircling one another with ties of love and caring, the Christian group should pray, "Deliver us from the evil one." One after another the members of the prayer group may share the times of testing they are experiencing, the need for strength they are feeling, and the lusts of the flesh troubling them now.

Knowing that moral peril does lurk in their future, the praying group commits their future to God's providential leading. "Lead us not into temptation" may often be filled in with specific requests as one member tells the group of a crucial decision he or she must make next week, and asks specifically for their prayers. A second member may be facing dishonesty down at the shop, another corruption in the office, another the military draft, or another the employer-corporation's scheming to exploit the poor. Still another may be tempted to the betrayal of purity in the home, or a breakdown in the love of neighbor. Intense and specific intercessory prayer may be accompanied by the laying on of hands as God's provision for victory over the evil one in all his wiles.

It is true that the loving heavenly Father is ever active, caring for and defending those who commit their lives to Him. Paul asserts that "the Lord is faithful; he will strengthen you and guard you from evil" (2 Thessalonians 3:3). But in verse one he humbly asks, strong leader that he is, that Christians should pray for him. Apparently God has somehow limited Himself to the prayer partnership of His people so that He is set free to do even more for someone when His partners-through-prayer pray to Him for a certain person. It is a mystery beyond all knowing that this should and could be so, but so the Scriptures imply, and so I believe. Prayers are indeed an added power for victory over evil and over the devil.

It is quite clear, I believe, that Paul set forward a Christian replacement for exorcism for Timothy to utilize in the pastoral care of the members of the congregation at Ephesus. He used a word, employed nowhere else in all of the New Testament, to describe this way to help members "escape from the snare of the devil, after being captured by him to do his will" (2 Timothy 2:26).

If any Christians might have been tempted to lapse back into animism, to say, "The devil made me do it,"

and to rely upon exorcism services to name and cast
devils out of one another, these converts were the most
likely to do so. The very air of Ephesus reeked with
superstitious fear of demons. The temple of Diana was
there and making idols of the Diana demon for every
household was big business. The labor force strongly
supported Diana worship, the source of their employ-
ment. They shouted for two hours in the marketplace,
"Great is Diana of the Ephesians" (Acts 19:28, KJV).
The leader of government—the town clerk—asserted
that Diana's supremacy could not be contradicted (Acts
19:36).

All the countervailing powers of the social structure—big labor, big capital, big church, and big government—were bound together by exorcism and its superstition. Every idea, assumption, and attitude was
permeated by it.

After the seven exorcist Sons of Sceva tried to bring
exorcism into the Jesus movement by adding, "I adjure
you by Jesus whom Paul preaches" (Acts 19:13), the
demons affirmed that they knew Jesus and Paul, but
tore the clothes from off the seven exorcists, so that they
fled naked and wounded.

Those who joined the Jesus movement, convicted by
all of this, brought their books of magic arts, exorcism,
and powwow—worth 50,000 pieces of silver—and
burned them. They had turned from a former way of
coping with evil spirits, but they certainly would be
looking for the Christian replacement for exorcism. This
Paul gives, point by point, in 2 Timothy 2:22-26. He
describes the brotherly way to help a believer to escape
from the demonic, from the snares of the devil.

Paul refers to the ensnared persons act of escaping from the devil's snare as *ana-napho,* getting awake again after a stupor, coming to reality again after a bad dream, becoming sober after being dead drunk. This word was commonly used to describe the sudden return to sobriety which a drunken person sometimes experiences when someone confronts him with responsibility.

Paul sees getting sober again about one's own responsibility as the act of escaping from Satan's snare. Paul is asserting that the Satan-ensnared person still has a free will and is responsible. The way to help the person is to awaken him to this responsibility.

To help a Satan-ensnared person reawaken to his or her responsibilities, Paul outlines attitudes which are essential for the helper. In 2 Timothy 2:21, he stresses purifying oneself from all that is ignoble, so that one's life is fit for the Master's use. He calls for maturity of personality, aligning oneself completely with God's program of peace, faith, love, and righteousness. This is in contrast to the immature pattern he describes as "youthful passions," by which he likely means such things as anger, expediency, use of force, and instability.

Paul urges a noncontroversial spirit, with a determination to stay out of hassles or quarrels. If the present clamor of disagreeing voices among exorcists and deliverance ministers is any sample, one can imagine the potential for arguments which Timothy faced as pastor of the Ephesus congregation. These members had burned their books of curious arts, it is true, but their minds were certainly still filled with ideas regarding what things were taboo, which acts were really occult, which objects to avoid, and which aspects of the old

magic were still to be feared. I can imagine that
Timothy, right in his own congregation, faced as great a
potential for disagreements, as great a diversity of
honest opinion, as I have found among the 50 or so
audiences I have lectured on exorcism!

Whereas exorcists usually take charge, take command, Paul urged Timothy to be "forbearing." This attitude allows the person to be totally free to decide. Just
as Jesus kept on loving the rich ruler as he walked away
in disobedience, so the forbearing helper sets the troubled person completely free, on his own, to say "yes" or
"no." The ensnared person senses that he is not being
subtly pressured. He does not need to say "yes" to avoid
rejection. He does not need to do what the helper-
teacher wants to gain his love and acceptance.

Some exorcists argue that the only people they deliver
are so possessed that their free will is no longer functioning at all; they have no free space left within which they
can decide anything; and, therefore, the exorcist stops
dealing with the person and his or her free will and deals
directly with the overpowering demon. I do not accept
this. I believe that because of the image of God within
man, God limits the devil's takeover, as He did for Job.
For this reason, I never bypass the person. This approach has succeeded on the back wards of mental hospitals in which I served, and with persons on whom all
the exorcists had given up. (I have also encountered
many persons who could receive little help.)

Paul insists that the helper remain always a kindly
teacher and, one might add, never an exorcist. Accustomed as the Ephesian converts were to exorcists as
the manipulators of the supernatural, Paul's dramatic

omission of an exorcist role doubtless impressed them very much.

It is worth mentioning, in passing, that teaching is one of the gifts of the Holy Spirit which the ascended Christ bestows to enable the church to function as His body. It is a highly honored charismatic enablement. Exorcism is conspicuously omitted in all the New Testament lists of gifts. This may be because exorcism is based upon the assumption that the person is helpless before Satan, can be totally possessed by him, and can alibi, "The devil made me do it." The exorcist always implicitly accepts this cop out, moves in to take over, and deals with the demon instead of the person.

Paul assumes that the helper-teacher will remain kind, forbearing, and gentle all the way through. He insists upon this repeatedly, and yet Paul admits that some "over-againstness," some confrontation, may be necessary. Paul speaks of correcting his opponent. The gentle teacher must be prepared for intense and sustained dialogue sessions.

Paul assumes that the wise teacher, who is helping an ensnared person to escape, will call up teachings from God's Word. He may cite warnings from God's deliverance from the demonic at the Exodus from Pharaoh. He may appeal to the victory cries from the psalms. He may thunder the warnings of God's prophets. He may point to Christ's once-for-all victory at Calvary. He may emphasize the real "Spirit possession" which happened at Pentecost. He may call for repentance from specific sins, alibis, evasions. He may point out the means of grace God has waiting for victory. He may call for confessing faults one to another

which is always the healing center of Christian fellowship. He will draw attention to the caring support group
of Christian friends waiting to encircle the suffering
person with their "deliver-us-from-the-evil-one" prayer.

The gentle teacher, who is helping an ensnared person
to escape, keeps relying upon Almighty God to grant
His miracle of repentance. Repentance is always
something God's holy love enables, even though it is
also an act of the person's responsible free will. Paul in-
jects the word *maypote* meaning "perhaps" (2 Timothy
2:25). There will always be mystery in that sacred inner
core of the human spirit where God's Spirit is calling to
repentance and the person's responsible free will is
deciding either to say "yes" or to say "no." Judas decided to say "no." We can only do our prayerful best
and then say, "God may perhaps grant that they will
repent and come to know the truth." The humble
teacher never guarantees that he can deliver ensnared
people. I doubt also that he should publish lists or startling stories of the demons he has named.

When the formerly ensnared person is being freed, it
is not as though an expert exorcist had named his demon
and sent it scurrying. The person is not thus left empty
and garnished, the ready victim for seven worse spirits
to reenter, as Christ warned might happen when the
exorcism method is used. The person is freed by "coming to know the truth." The helper has been a teacher.
Solid truth has been injected. New insights have been
gained. The helped person is filled with some new understanding, some new wisdom, a solid foundation for future victory. He has grasped some new facts to work
with. He has discovered some new potential strengths

within himself which he now can claim and use in gaining new victories.

I have constantly protested the telling of demon-naming stories, and the building up of a theology of pastoral care by the use of deliverance ministry exorcism stories. So I must restrain myself when the method which I feel the Apostle Paul outlined as the replacement for exorcism has been utilized, and some good results have been achieved. I will not pad my book with a lot of repentance and faith victory stories either. (I have had some failures too.)

However, I simply must report just one of the many times I used Paul's method outlined above. The young man was a Black Panther from Detroit's gangland. He had been on hard drugs for a long time, into Satan worship, and all the rest. Exorcists with their "I adjure you in the name of Jesus" or "I command you in the name of Jesus" approach had tried to cast his demons from him. Each time it seemed seven worse demons took control. He spoke in tongues both when high in church and when high on hard drugs and busy planning violence.

I remember conferring with his psychiatrist, a Christian doctor who had served an overseas mission field for many years before taking up his psychiatric residency. We agreed together on ways to work against the young man's suicidal tendencies by keeping him in dialogue with one of us.

The young man had been keeping a diary of his chaotic nightmares. He had been writing down his bizarre plans for violent takeover of this or that establishment. As an act of his repentance before God, I challenged him to give me that diary, and to quit writing his plans for violence. He did so. His recovery began. Later, during one of the many quiet walks he and I had on the mental hospital grounds, he told me that my quiet faith that God could help him to repent had been the turning point.

For Additional Reading and Reference

Adams, Jay E. *Competent to Counsel* (Grand Rapids: Baker Book House, 1970).

Barclay, William. *Letters to Timothy, Titus, and Philemon* (Philadelphia: Westminster Press, 1960).

Bender, Harold. *These Are My People* (Scottdale, Pa.: Herald Press, 1962).

Bender, Ross. *The People of God* (Scottdale, Pa.: Herald Press, 1971).

Christenson, Larry. *A Charismatic Approach to Social Action* (Minneapolis: Bethany Fellowship, 1974).

Frazier, Claude, ed. *Faith Healing: Finger of God? or Scientific Curiosity?* (New York: Thomas Nelson, 1973).

Hiebert, D. Edmond. *Second Timothy* (Chicago: Moody Press, 1958).

Howe, Ruel L. *The Miracle of Dialogue* (New York: Seabury, 1963).

Jeschke, Marlin. *Discipling the Brother* (Scottdale, Pa.: Herald Press, 1972).

Rose, Louis. *Faith Healing* (New York: Penguin, 1971).

11
Praise Also Helps

Long ago I discovered that God wanted to save His people without their needing to fight if they would obey Him, start praising Him for victory awhile, and then stand still and see the salvation of the Lord. This is the heart of the Exodus victory over Pharaoh and all his exorcists, idol-demons, and enslaving institutions. Moses commanded, "See the salvation of the Lord. . . . The Egyptians whom you see today, you shall never see again. . . . The Lord will fight for you, and you have only to stand still" (Exodus 14:13, 14).

Especially in defensive wars, when Israel was being attacked by her enemies, God promised victory by "holy war." Israel was not to rely upon armies. Her survival as a people depended upon God alone, and upon His readiness and ability to intervene by any kind of miracle needed. Israel demonstrated her trust in Jehovah's sovereignty over any enemy or evil demon by praising God, in advance, for the victory He was sure to give. I concluded that resisting the snares of the evil one and of evil, whether personalized or not, was certainly a defensive battle.

God's way of victory was not by the usual sources of safety. Samuel pleaded with Israel not to rely upon armies with their skillfully trained violence, nor in kings so prone to deify themselves. Samuel promised, "He will guard the feet of his faithful ones . . . for not by might shall a man prevail" (1 Samuel 2:9). This theme of an early prophet, Samuel, was emphasized repeatedly by God's spokesmen and reasserted by a later prophet, Zechariah: "Not by might, nor by power, but by my Spirit, says the Lord of hosts" (4:6). Victory comes by a calm reliance upon God's power, God's Spirit, God's presence, God's protection, and God's providential leading and commitment to His people.

A crisis for God's people was a call to start praising, in advance, for the victory they knew He would bring. The first acts of defense were to pray, to organize the choirs for praise, and to start shouting the victory shout.

What God's preacher-prophets promised so often, the sovereign God performed again and again. God drove out enemies by His angel in Exodus 23:23, by His terror in Exodus 23:27, and by hornets in Exodus 23:28.

This victory pattern occurred repeatedly in the life of Israel. As God's people began praising Him, as they started their trumpeters blasting out the victories, God gave His people miraculous deliverance. Under Joshua, He gave them the city of Jericho (Joshua 6); under Gideon, He delivered them from the Midianites (Judges 7); and under Asa, He defeated an Ethiopian army many times the strength of Israel (2 Chronicles 14:11).

Apparently, brutal and destructive wars were part of God's punishment upon His people for their refusal to be guided only by God's prophets and protected only by

His "holy war." Because the Israelites insisted upon relying upon kings, with conscripted armies and chariots of iron, they often found themselves caught in stupid, senseless, and destructive wars which resulted in the slaughter of many of their people.

The ideal "holy war" (victory by praising in advance) is pictured in 2 Chronicles 20. When a massive, overwhelming enemy attacked, King Jehoshaphat feared the Lord, prayed, and called God's people to prayer and fasting (v. 3). The people assembled for worship and prayer. They recited God's victories in their past. Entire families, including wives and little children, stood at attention before the Lord (v. 13). It was actually a service of worship.

God gave a prophetic word, the fresh assurance of His victory (v. 17), with the explicit instruction to stand still and see God's victory. The king and people fell down in worship as the choirs arose to begin their anthems of praise.

God's people were admonished by their king to believe the prophets (v. 20). Additional choirs were appointed and they marched toward the enemy singing, "Give thanks to the Lord, for his steadfast love endures for ever" (v. 21). The whole procession was much like a jubilee celebration when God's people marched to the temple for worship.

As always in "holy war," God Himself gave the total victory, without His people fighting. They assembled as victors in the valley of Beracah (blessing) and returned as one great choir procession—with trumpets, harps, and lyres playing—back to the temple of the Lord from which they had marched out originally (v. 28).

This classic pattern is repeated in Hezekiah's "holy war" victory over Sennacherib (2 Chronicles 32) and in Elisha's victory over the Syrians (2 Kings 6). Again and again God made good His promise given in Deuteronomy 28:7, "The Lord will cause your enemies who rise against you to be defeated before you; they shall come out against you one way, and flee before you seven ways."

Regrettably, the "holy war" way of victory by praising in advance was lost in Israel after they relied on kings, conscripted armies, and weaponry. But praise as a way of victory continues on through both Testaments.

As I was working on the manuscript for this book, I was asking myself how the above observations relate to victory over the demonic. I met Judson Cornwall at a conference and he shared with me his experience. He tells it briefly also in his book, *Let Us Praise* (pp. 71, 72).

Judson had been busy in a deliverance ministry, naming and casting out demons from troubled people, and casting demons out of buildings. He experienced the downward spiral of gloom, pessimism, and defeat which I have noticed so often in the exorcists I have known. His experience in praising God and turning away from exorcism corroborated my own convictions.

God warned Judson that the naming of demons is actually the kind of attention the perverted father of lies seeks, and that naming demons is not the way God desires for His people.

God led Judson to study the place of "praise in advance" throughout the Scriptures. He has used it with good effects in many congregations and conferences.

God evidently honors "praise for victory in advance"

as a down-to-earth way of victory for troubled and Satan-ensnared persons. God implies this in Psalm 81 which begins with commands to praise, and goes on in verse 9 to promise, "there shall be no strange god [demon]among you." Even when God's people sensed their failures after hearing God's law read and expounded, and wanted only to mourn and weep, Ezra insisted that "the joy of the Lord is your strength" and that praise is one of the ways to victory. I recall a number of charismatic conferences I have attended over the years and remember that the sessions devoted to exorcism and related subjects left a sense of gloom and pessimism. In contrast to this, the mighty praise anthems like "Praise God from Whom All Blessing Flow" left a residue of joy and strength.

More and more I find that, as I start to praise God for His past mercies, He becomes my present salvation in the anxiety of the moment. I intend to continue in this way of victory because I believe it is profoundly biblical, wholesome psychologically, and effective practically.

But what shall I do when I don't feel like praising God? What motivations can I rely upon to start me praising God, even while I am being tested and tried? If I have a trusting Father-child relationship with my God, then that trust enables me to believe that somehow He will help all things to work together for my good. I can start to give thanks awhile for any and all things, if I really trust my Father's providential love and rely in childlike faith upon His power.

Likely Paul had preached often, in the hearing of Silas his co-worker, that all things work together for good for the Christian. Paul taught that one can learn to be content and at peace in whatever state one finds oneself. He stressed that a believer can bring all prayers and supplications to God with thanksgiving and praise. These triumphant certainties surged to the surface within Paul even when his back was bleeding in the jail at Philippi. At midnight, in spite of sore backs, Paul and Silas praised God. God's power was released anew. They were delivered from their enemies. The praise way to victory had worked again. Deeply held convictions tend to surge to the surface in times of trauma.

This is not a take-it-or-leave-it matter. God has commanded praise, even though I may not always feel like declaring the praises of Him who called me out of darkness into His marvelous light (1 Peter 2:9). One of God's purposes in calling out a people peculiarly His own—a holy nation as it were, a people with priestly compassion for all who suffer—is that they might declare God's praise.

God not only desires our praise, but He knows that we need to praise. It is necessary for our honesty. Praise is necessary to keep gratitude alive in our souls and to counteract our basic selfishness. Praise is needed to keep us optimistic in our outlook. Praise is needed for our mental health. Praise satisfies a basic desire we have to celebrate.

Many of the psalms, and most of the epistles of the New Testament, retell God's acts, praising Him for His deeds of grace, and reciting what He has done for man. One of the greatest things any congregation can do to help members find victory over ensnaring evil is to vitalize their praise, to intensify their praise, to pour more emotion and power into their praise, to seek for more freedom of God's Holy Spirit in praise, until members feel they are actually joining with the church triumphant in exalted praise around the throne of God in heaven.

For Additional Reading and Reference:

Boom, Corrie Ten. *The Hiding Place* (Old Tappan, N.J.: Chosen Books, 1971).

Carothers, Merlin R. *Prison to Praise* (Plainfield: Logos International, 1970).

Christenson, James. *Contemporary Worship Services* (Old Tappan, N.J.: Revell, 1971).

Cornwall, Judson. *Let Us Praise* (Plainfield, N.J.: Logos, 1973).

Lind, Millard. *Biblical Foundation for Christian Worship* (Scottdale, Pa.: Herald Press, 1973).

Reid, Clyde. *Celebrate the Temporary* (New York: Harper & Row, 1972).

Watkin, Keith. *Liturgies in a Time When Cities Burn* (New York: Abingdon, 1969).

White, James F. *New Forms of Worship* (New York: Abingdon, 1971).

12

Possession by the Holy Spirit Prevents Possession by the Unholy One

People often asked me, after my lectures on exorcism, whether a person filled with the Holy Spirit could at the same time be possessed by demons. Having read scores of books and pamphlets written by deliverance ministers and exorcists, I know that a great many say "yes" to this question. Many of these are also charismatics, at one time stressing their joy and ecstasy from Spirit fullness, and again admitting that they periodically need to have demons identified within them and cast from them.

The question came again one day, with fear and anguish, from a college student after my second lecture on exorcism given on her campus. "Can I, a Spirit-filled Christian, find myself possessed by a demon?" she asked.

As nearly as I can recall, I answered, "Yes, in the same way your brain can be blown with delirium tremens. Delirium tremens will not get you, however, unless you choose to drink alcohol, repeatedly, persistently, and in spite of knowledge you are hurting your brain. You will have other warnings first. In much the same way, if you grieve the Holy Spirit, persist in known sin, cater to the occult against better knowledge, and go on and on in this way, you could become 'possessed.' Satan has to secure both God's permission and yours before he can possess you."

Demon possession is not a rapid, unpredictable takeover by the unholy spirit of the body of someone who has been habitually living in the fellowship and power of God's Holy Spirit. The two realms are so opposite that a lot happens between those two conditions.

Questions like these reveal that some people place the Holy Spirit and the unholy spirit (demons) on the same level. They assume that evenly-matched spirits are seeking to gain possession of every person. Possession by one is just as likely as possession by the other. The ready inference is that exorcism is the way to manipulate the supernatural in favor of the Holy Spirit rather than the unholy spirit. This is dualism, pure and simple. These assumptions do not flow from a strong monotheism.

These assumptions of dualism would fit readily into many of the non-Christian religions of the world, but the biblical view is different. God's Holy Spirit moves on a different plane, and with far greater power, than the unholy spirit. Contrast, rather than comparison, is called for.

According to the Bible, God's Spirit has been creating from the dawn of time until now, in sovereign goodness. The unholy spirit is pictured as a spoiler, a destroyer of creation, a creature bent upon wrecking, a devourer seeking whom he may consume, a serpent, and a subtle beast.

The Holy Spirit broods creatively over God's world, ever shaping, forming beauty, designing for man's good and God's glory. The unholy spirit has often been seen by Christian leaders as chaos, as void, as form destroying, as nothingness. It is limited to mimicking. It can only react and be parasitic. It is not a creator in the way God is Creator.

According to the Scriptures, God's Spirit comes to man in community, to the two or three gathered in His name, to the fellowship as a whole. When the elders of the congregation lay hands on the sick for healing, all of the congregation are with those hands in their loving touch, focusing their combined powers of intercessory prayers upon the suffering member. Every member in the body of Christ, the fellowship created by common sharing in the Holy Spirit, seeks to mediate the love and power of Jesus Christ, the Head of the body, to the body member who is hurting. This is one of the ways God's Holy Spirit blesses in and through community.

In contrast, the unholy spirit seems to work in loneliness, friendlessness, alienation, separation, and estrangement, and the feeling that one's hand is set against every other man's.

When a young man, shattered by what he claimed were 62 LSD trips, pleaded with me to go with him to the lonely bedroom where he usually hid away in his stupor, I did not name demons and cast them out. This would have appealed to him because he declared that he saw demon-snakes crawling out of every knothole in the paneled ceiling of his bedroom.

Rather, I relied upon the stronger Spirit of God who indwelt his parents and his former friends down at the youth group at the church. I stayed with him to comfort him a long while myself, and later helped to get him ac-

cepted back into the caring youth fellowship from which
he had strayed. God's loving Spirit triumphed in his life
in the same superior way that light expels darkness.
God's Holy Spirit overcomes the unholy spirit.

The young man is fully healed, living a wholesome life
again. God's Spirit does miracles, but not to provide a
spectacle for onlookers. God's Spirit is constantly making a total assault upon evil, so that every healing is part
of a larger victory design. Every healing is a sign pointing to God's larger intention of giving life, renewing life,
providing the more abundant life, and resurrecting the
individual to eternal life. In absolute contrast to this, the
unholy spirit sometimes is able to mimic God with deceptive marvels, signs which are confusing, and which
seem opposed to God's usual laws. Paul warned the
Thessalonian congregation of "the lawless one" who
performs deceptive marvels (2 Thessalonians 2:9). Any
signs and wonders God's Holy Spirit does are to witness
to the truth (Hebrews 2:4), to confirm the preached
word (Romans 15:19), and to authenticate the presence
of the loving God in the midst of His people (2 Corinthians 12:12). When testing whether a spirit is God's
Spirit, or an unholy spirit, one must watch carefully
whether laws God has given are respected.

God's Holy Spirit witnesses to truth, to truth as
represented by all Jesus said and did, and by truth as the
prophets and apostles were inspired to give it in the
Scriptures. The unholy spirit authors confusion. He is a
liar and the father of lies. His efforts result in discord,
incoherence, absurdity, and in manifestations that are
inconsistent with what Jesus said and did. When I need
to identify the spirits tugging at my own spirit, I can

rather quickly test them by all I know about Jesus.

As I understand it, God's Holy Spirit convicts, lovingly reasoning with men about God's right way to live and the inevitable judgment to come if persons refuse God's holy will. The unholy spirit nags, confuses, accuses, blames, and induces feelings of worthlessness, anger, hopelessness, and despair. As a counselee tells me his feelings, I can usually detect whether he is hearing God's loving call, or whether the accuser of the brethren is at work.

Paul Tournier, a psychiatrist who counsels from a frankly Christian point of view, has written an entire volume, *Guilt and Grace,* that traces the nagging, uneasy, self-condemning, guilty feeling which failing persons experience apart from God's grace. He reports the ways in which man seeks to excuse himself, to defend himself, to repress his guilt feelings, to pay for what he has done wrong, and to judge the same failing in others. In contrast to this, God's freely given grace tends to set the guilty person free. Forgiveness in advance invites the prodigal to come home, because God loves persons even while they are sinners.

God's gracious Spirit works to free people from guilt feelings that press in upon them because they have broken a taboo of an earlier authority figure. God's Spirit seeks to free people from a neurotic guilt they carry along because of sex feelings and desires, and seeks rather to convict and to call them lovingly away from any actual misuse of sex. A minister with whom I counseled was able to bid good-bye, by God's grace, to a long nagging guilt about masturbation, as he accepted God's forgiveness and covenanted with God to use his sex drives in wholesome ways the rest of his life.

God's gracious Spirit is continually seeking to rescue us from disgrace, to reestablish our sense of being forgiven, loved, received back, restored to relationships with God, and set free from bondage. While God's gracious Holy Spirit has access to us always, the unholy spirit can get at us only if God allows it and if we allow it. God gives the Holy Spirit to those who ask Him (Luke 11:13), but persons must choose to reject God before the unholy spirit gets his best chance.

God's Spirit works to regenerate whereas the unholy one degenerates. God's Spirit produces genuine saints but the unholy spirit only hypocrites. God's Spirit distributes gifts that enable us to do Christ's loving deeds in our needy world. The unholy spirit leads persons away from concrete acts of doing justly, loving mercy and kindness, and walking humbly and transparently before both God and man. Jesus saw Satan fall like lightning from heaven as He watched the simple, honest, nameless seventy going out in lives of lowly witness (Luke 10:18).

I believe that God's Holy Spirit links up with God's image implanted in man. God's Spirit speaks both below the level of consciousness and above it, through intuition as well as logic, through emotion as well as reason, to the very ground of man's being, the depths from which spring the very issues of life. In contrast, the unholy spirit has not created man and implanted his unholy image in the same way God has done. Satan's seductions come as something alien, untrue, false to the image of God within man, clashing with man's profoundest hopes, making sense only to man in his fallenness, his prodigal posture away from his father's house.

In my own life, and in the lives of counselees I seek to help, the supreme proof of the Holy Spirit's presence is the fruit of the Spirit. The Holy Spirit produces love, the unholy one discord. The Holy Spirit brings joy and the unholy one moroseness. God's Spirit produces peace and long-suffering, gentleness, goodness, and faith. The fallen angels are always pictured as helpless and defeated before the power of God, His good angels, and His Holy Spirit. The fruit of the Spirit within the individual Christian counteracts Satan's attack through the lusts of the flesh.

For Additional Reading and Reference:

Bridge, Donald, and Phypers, David. *Spiritual Gifts and the Church* (Downers Grove: Inter-Varsity Press, 1973).

Drescher, John M. *Spirit Fruit* (Scottdale, Pa.: Herald Press, 1974).

DuPlessis, David J. *The Spirit Bade Me Go: A Famous Pentecostal Tells His Story* (Plainfield, N.J.: Logos, 1970).

Hamilton, Michael, ed. *The Charismatic Movement* (Grand Rapids: Eerdmans, 1975).

Kraus, C. Norman. *The Community of the Spirit* (Grand Rapids: Eerdmans, 1974).

Peterson, Mary. *Healing, A Spiritual Adventure* (Philadelphia: Fortress, 1974).

Riffel, Herman H. *A Living, Loving Way: Christian Maturity and the Spirit's Power* (Minneapolis: Bethany Fellowship, 1973).

Sherrill, John L. *They Speak with Other Tongues* (Old Tappan, N.J.: Chosen Books, 1965).

13

The Big Demons (Principalities and Powers) Oppress Me Most

Paul declared that our wrestling against demons is not primarily against the little "flesh-and-blood" demons, such as the demon of anger I give place to when I allow the sun to go down upon my wrath (Ephesians 4:26, 27). He reminded the congregation at Ephesus that our wrestling is really against the "big demons," the principalities and powers, against the world rulers of this present darkness, against the spiritual hosts of wickedness in heavenly places (Ephesians 6:12). What does this really mean?

Many people think of the hosts of wickedness in heavenly places as discarnate imps, swarms of little demons like the flies or locusts of Egypt, floating invisibly through the air, seen as rarely as flying saucers, but always seeking to get into someone's body. Somehow the Christian is called to wrestle against these demon-swarms. To chase out these demon-swarms some deliverance ministers conduct exorcisms of buildings, of sanctuaries before a service of worship, or of haunted houses. The deliverance ministers of some non-Christian religions try to suck the demon out through body openings, to drive the demon out by brutal whippings, to smoke the demon out with incense, to scare the demon out with eerie noises, and to move the demon out by denouncing it and commanding it to depart in the name of a superior spirit power. Many exorcists use dances or employ amulets and charms. Some inflict pain, drink blood, or examine entrails of animals. Others use mixtures of oil and water. But common to most exorcism rituals is the belief that swarms of invisible gnat-like demons are always present and can enter the body.

I think there is a better and truer interpretation of the principalities and powers against which we are called to do our primary wrestling. According to this view, kingdoms of evil are formed when and where a proud, rebellious, strong leader gets into a place of power so that he can create structures of oppression, and from this center of institutionalized power, works against the kingdom of God. A "principality and power" is a block of influence which should be under God's guidance, since it is part of God's creation, but is now organized to function without seeking God's will, and actually works against God.

The first tempter in Eden began to try to organize cohorts into a systematized rebellion against God. As an original "Antichrist," he was trying to get evil and rebellion into organized form. He was trying to form a principality and power.

As God's people came to view the demonic opposition that oppressed them in Egypt, it was not the little demons of gnats, flies, frogs, or hail that they worried about at the time, or sang about afterward in their psalms, victory songs, and hymns of deliverance. The real demon was Pharaoh the king. Pharaoh had developed a mythology that he was a deity. His exorcists and magicians helped him pull off his dirty tricks. From his kingdom of evil he worked against the will of God, enslaved the poor, and withstood God's prophet. The deliverance hymns and psalms of Israel were always clear that the real demon was King Pharaoh, and God's victory was over him.

The prophets had the same view. They seldom mentioned the little demons, whether of Egypt's plagues, or flesh and blood demons such as modern exorcists are busy combatting. Several prophets had warned that if Israel went down the world's way of choosing kings, their kings would become demonic. Their kings would turn into exploiters and oppressors. They would build around themselves kingdoms which would not really serve God, but would serve the king and his inflated ego. For the prophets the very institution of kingship tended to be demonic.

Isaiah promised that, in time of genuine repentance, Israel would recognize this tendency of oppressor kings to become demons. In Isaiah 14:3-23 he helped God's people to jeer at the king of Babylon. They scoffed at the way he deified himself, building up the usual myth that he was divine, that he had come down from heaven, and that his throne was part of the universal rule of the gods. His attempt to make himself like the Most High (v. 14) will fail, they predicted. He will be cast down to Sheol. History will stare in amazement at the way the self-deified king of Babylon has fallen and crashed into disgrace. All this actually came to pass.

It should be noted, in passing, that not until the time

of Origen, who developed the allegorical way of interpreting Scripture, did God's people think of spiritualiz-
ing this passage, taking its real meaning away from the
literal king of Babylon, and making it describe an
original fall of an almost almighty devil from heaven.

Entirely too many sincere expositors, in their dualistic
attempt to explain the beginning of Satan's primevial
sovereignty, copy Origen's allegory and misuse the
prophet's message to the king of Babylon. The allegorical method is always risky.

The king of Tyre had deified himself also, as
practically all monarchs did, by building a god-myth
about himself. His self-built myth traced his origins to
creation, to the garden of Eden, the holy mountain of
God, where he reigned with a cherub as his anointed se-
curity guard. Ezekiel 28 debunks the king's deity-myth
and shows that the king of Tyre is really a demonic principality and power, an enemy system set against God's
kingdom. These prophets were united in seeing the
kingship self-deification myths, with the resultant
divine-right-of-kings, as the real demon, the real principality and power.

In the temptations hurled against Christ, the "subtle
beast" tempter gave scant attention to the little flesh and
blood demons of pride, self-centeredness, or bodily appetite. The great temptation was to set up a principality
and power, to gather self-deifying myths of greatness as
earth's kings usually did, and to create structures of influence, power, and oppression. Just as Christ's own
awareness of His powers as God's Son were shaping in
His mind, Satan was seducing Him toward setting up an
organization apart from the will and way of God

Almighty. He was tempted to establish a principality and power, which would have been in opposition to the kingdom of His Father God. So Jesus felt it, and as such He withstood it.

When the congregation at Ephesus first read Paul's letter reminding them that the attention of their congregational meeting should be primarily upon the principalities and powers (Ephesians 6:12), I believe their minds automatically went to the interlocking structures of oppression and evil which blighted the lives of all who dwelt in Ephesus. Full well they knew that the organized religion, organized government, organized industry, and organized labor of the city were all equally devoted to Diana worship. They knew that Demetrius, in just one meeting of the craftsmen, could start a riot—a surging, insane, violent mob (Acts 19:32), most of whom did not really understand what they were yelling about. Even so Christians must be realistic when they find themselves in a volatile situation, in which passions are easily inflamed, and when violence can erupt in an hour.

The members of the Ephesus congregation could look out the front window of their humble house-church and see outlined against the heavens the majestic temple to Diana. It was one of the seven wonders of the world. In it was a sacred stone, which was said to had fallen down out of the heavens from Jupiter. In front of the temple were 117 pillars, one set there by each government of the civilized world, offering tribute to the great Diana. Around the temple hovered a highly organized and ruthless priesthood, who saw to it that the superstitious myths of their demon-deity were kept alive. Their traveling exorcists likely collected fees, along with the idols-images of Diana they sold, to manipulate the demon world for the poor superstitious masses. They warned of Diana's vengeance if protection-fees were not forthcoming. They kept the level of fear high, shielding the masses from any other possible world-view. No wonder the apostle could refer to "this present darkness."

Paul wanted the Ephesian Christians to discuss together how they, individually in their daily work and as a group founding a Christian congregation, were really wrestling against the all-pervasive influences, ideas, assumptions, attitudes, power structures, and organizations set up by the oppressive Diana system. Gaius and Aristarchus could tell how they had been dragged into the theater by the mob the day the demonstrators went beserk in the streets (Acts 19:29). Members could discuss the ways in which the news was managed and slanted to favor the Diana myth, how the teachers supported the system, until every value and assumption by which people made their daily decisions was twisted.

I imagine the Ephesian congregation discussed how they could keep their children from imbibing the patriotisms of Ephesus. Could Christians work in an industry whose end product was an idol of Diana? Could they honestly pay their taxes when they knew the most of the money was channeled (by the coalition government chaired by the town clerk) into projects that further oppressed the poor, kept them in ignorance and superstition, favored the wealthy silversmiths, and benefited the corporations that profited by the Diana myth? The congregation needed to stand together against the wily, subtle influences of the sin-filled system. In their prayerful discussions, they were wrestling against the powers.

Some, remembering that handkerchiefs of Paul's had been taken out and used to cast out individual flesh and blood demons (Acts 19:11), possibly felt that a ministry of exorcism would be a way they could stand together against the principalities and powers. But the Ephesus elders, who had met with Paul a year later at Miletus (Acts 20:17-38), recalled that Paul had ignored his exorcism ministry altogether as he reviewed his work among them. He described in detail what he had tried to do among them, and conspicuously omitted any mention at all of exorcism, either his own or the abortive attempt of the seven sons of Sceva.

I believe that the Christian congregation is called to discern, stand together, and wrestle against the principalities and powers of their own culture and of their own town. This will vary in every congregation according to the way evil permeates the structures of the life of their community. A congregation meeting in Chicago cannot very realistically wrestle against the organized hate of Protestants and Catholics in Belfast, Ireland. Perhaps they can have some influence through their prayers, pleas, protests, and even letters of encouragement to congregations in Belfast. But they can wrestle against religious bigotry nearer home. They can enter Christ-honoring dialogue between Protestants and Catholics in Bible study groups, or conversations at various levels. They are not completely free from the command to wrestle against powers, even at a distance.

If the Chicago congregation is really to wrestle against organized evil, oppressive systems of ideas and of power, they may need to wrestle with city hall for justice for the poor of their area; against the system of dope pushers which is helping to seduce and blight youth; against organized crime which makes their streets unsafe at night; against the John Birch Society with their activities and ideas to promote hate and discrimination; against the recruitment of their youth for service in a military machine which can turn their sons into persons capable of committing a My-Lai massacre; against a scientism and naturalism in the schools which studies God's world of nature and history as if God has not been active in it. All of these represent evil in organized form, oppressing persons who would live their full and free obedience to Jesus Christ.

The big demons do oppress me the most, and yet I find it hard to suggest ways congregations should be wrestling against the principalities and powers, and Antichrist systems of their area. Paul told the young pastor Timothy to watch out for leaders who are deceiving and being deceived (2 Timothy 3:13). But I want to avoid any heresy hunts, any McCarthyism by the church.

The witchcraft trials by the Puritan church leaders at Salem are of interest in this regard. Some of the church leaders who called for the torture of witches were apparently as bewitched as the witches themselves. The God-fearing Calvinistic Puritans, studying their Scriptures and saying their prayers, functioned as demons worse than the most active witches. The fact that government sanctioned this excess of the church only made the whole coalition a more horrible host of wickedness in high places (Ephesians 6:12). Government approval did not absolve the Puritan leaders from the crimes they committed in torturing a poor, frightened woman to death.

What are some ways sincere Christians seek to wrestle against the principalities and powers? Many deliverance ministers feel they are doing so when they expel, one by one, little demons which have gotten into Christians from the demon swarms which fill the air. One published list of expelled demons includes gluttony, nicotine, masturbation, giggling, laziness, gossip, silliness, loneliness, and so on through 150 more.[1] Glenna Henderson, describing the casting out of her demons amidst considerable vomiting, found them to be named self-pity, sex fantasy, crossed-eyes, Littimus, adulterous spirit, convulsive Reuben, and Charlie-named-after-a-king.[2] I respect the sincerity of these Christians, but I cannot believe that such casting out of flesh and blood demons is either a good application of Ephesians 6, nor is it good for Christian victorious living.

Herman Riffle, in his book *A Living, Loving Way,* tells of a black woman pastor who "sent her people out into the riot area and took authority over the evil forces that caused the people to hate each other, in that way quieting the area around her church." That impresses me as a courageous way for a congregation to wrestle with spiritual wickedness in high places.

Several Roman Catholic and Protestant pastors in Denver have banded together in an appeal to churches to remove all symbols of competing loyalties, such as national flags, from their sanctuaries. When I reflect upon the demonic things nationalism and patriotism can do, remembering that clergymen were so carried along with patriotism that they placed Hitler's picture on their church altars even as he was beginning the murder of 6 million Jews—then I can see how these pastors feel they must wrestle against the principalities and powers of patriotism.

The congregation is called to do more than sit back and rejoice when a Watergate trial has exorcized a few demons of corruption from a few high offices of government. William Stringfellow, in his book *An Ethic for Christians and Other Aliens in a Strange World,* feels that the pouring of napalm, the same kind used to burn innocent children in helpless Vietnamese villages, upon a collection of army draft records, was a mighty act of exorcism. It is always easier to identify the demonic when it is far away, beyond our reach, and after the testing light of history is upon it all.

Sincere, concerned Christians disagree widely on what the present-day principalities and powers are which the congregation must stand against. Looking back it is easy to identify the demonic in the power of the Emperor Nero, the periods of corruption in the papacy, the horrible crusades, the Thirty Years' War, the Inquisition, the witch trials of Salem, the racism of Hitler, the activities of the Ku-Klux Klan, the riots of hate and violence in the streets, or the Protestant-Catholic war in Ireland.

Getting closer home, some would identify as demonic a godless communism, and others an equally godless capitalism. Some would see demonic principalities in the military-industrial complex of Washington, D.C. Some see it in the apartheid of South Africa, and some in protests and riots over busing in Boston; some in slum landlords who exploit the poor; some in the Mafia; some in monopolistic business; and some in self-serving labor unions. Hendrik Berkhof, in his very helpful book *Christ and the Powers,* believes that demonic "mam-

mon" can be reduced to necessary finances, and a demonic "ism" like Nazism to a mere idea still around but
not powerful enough any longer to destroy.

In every area there will be oppressive, organized evil.
In every community the congregation must run some
risk if they raise their voices against entrenched wrong.
There seems always to be a Demetrius (as there was
among the silversmiths of Ephesus) who is ready to in-
cite a riot if the church challenges the sinful status quo.

An attorney and theologian from France, Jacques
Ellul, in his book *The New Demons,* lists the newly
threatening "demons" as the subtle, all-persuasive
power of scientism, sex, materialism, consumerism, indi-
vidualism, or blind nationalism.

If each congregation will actually attempt to be faithful in its own situation, to take what loving and courageous action they can against the demonic powers
around them, I believe God's Spirit will overrule for the
glory of His name and the defeat of the principalities
and powers. Paul dared to believe that God will show
His wisdom, through the church and her faithfulness, to
the watching principalities and powers (Ephesians 3:10).
God intends to incorporate even their rebellion into His
final victory.

All principalities and powers are part of God's creation, Paul reminds us in Colossians 1:16. Christ has already disarmed the principalities and powers, he adds in
2:15. Christ will take care of the enemy if His people will
follow the Spirit's leading in every decision. As in God's
"holy war" under Joshua, God's people should spend a
lot of time praising God for His victories in the past,
simply obey in the present, with the best leading His

Spirit gives them, and God through His overruling
providence will do the rest.

For Additional Reading and Reference:

Berkhof, Hendrik. *Christ and the Powers* (Scottdale, Pa.:
    Herald Press, 1962).
Come, Arnold B. *Agents of Reconciliation* (Philadelphia:
    Westminster Press, 1964).
Ellul, Jacques. *The New Demons* (New York: Seabury,
    1975).
Hulme, William E. *Two Ways of Caring: A Biblical
    Design for Balanced Ministry* (Minneapolis: Augs-
    burg, 1973).
Montgomery, John W. *Principalities and Powers* (Min-
    neapolis: Bethany Fellowship, 1973).
Philpot, Kent. *A Manual of Demonology and the Occult*
    (Grand Rapids: Zondervan, 1973).
Rose, Stephen C., ed. *Who's Killing the Church*
    (Chicago: City Missionary Society, 1966).
Sharp, Gene. *The Methods of Nonviolent Action* (Boston:
    Porter Sargent, 1974).
Yoder, John H. *The Politics of Jesus* (Grand Rapids:
    Eerdmans, 1972).

14

Vital Life Within Christ's Church Is My Strongest Defense

One reason the Jews could live so free from evil spirits, even while surrounded by superstitious neighbors busy with exorcisms, was the fact that God made a "people" out of them. God worked to mold them into a strong-knit group, with intense ties of belonging, many ways to support one another, a strong sense of being for one another, and a tremendous feeling of being "we." They recited a common history, studied common laws, followed common dietary standards, and had common concerns about sanitation and ecology. They had common ways of relating to ancestors, coping with tragedy, and aiding the helpless. They shared common rituals, beliefs, and worship, common hopes and sense of destiny. They had common ways of dealing with the deviant, solemnizing life's milestones, and standing against group disruption. When they obeyed God most fully, they were most truly a close-knit people.

In working with persons who feel they are demon possessed, and in discussing and reading about such cases, I have discovered that demonized individuals have one thing in common. They usually feel they are outsiders and that they don't quite belong. They feel alienated and estranged and suffer intensely from it. They feel ostracized, unclean, and unloved. In desperation, they panic and strike out blindly.

Reports of exorcisms among Roman Catholics reveal that many of those afflicted are nuns, who feel lonely, unloved, and left out of the changes which are coming in the church. In the biblical records, the man ostracized until he lived among the tombs was certainly "out of it." The Syrophoenician woman felt like an outsider.

I am convinced that Jesus intended to create a new "people." He said that the Spirit of Jehovah was on Him to proclaim "jubilee year," the acceptable year of the Lord (Luke 4:16-21). Jubilee was to be the year when all debts were forgiven, all relationships righted, all enslaved people set free, and when "loving peoplehood" as God intended would get a new start once more (Leviticus 25:10-16). Christ's critics jeered at the "friend of publican and sinners" stance He took. They never quite understood why the common people heard Him so gladly.

Jesus hoped that persons who joined His movement would discover in glad amazement that they had inherited fathers, mothers, brothers, sisters, houses, and lands a hundredfold. He hoped His disciples would become brothers and sisters with Him in the family of His heavenly Father. He intended that countless acts of tender, loving care would unite the disciple group. Members of the group would be constantly giving the cup of cold water, washing one another's feet in humble service, discovering afterward that the lowliest act was as if "you did it to me" (Matthew 25:40). Jesus taught them to have a common purse, to enjoy breaking bread together, to bring their quarrels honestly into the open, and to talk together about things that really mattered.

When the Holy Spirit's work increased in the new movement of Pentecost, the "we spirit" grew. People felt that all they owned was really for the sake of the group. Differences of background gave way before the new reality of a oneness in God, a common union in sharing His life, a common filling with His power, a common sense of priorities, a common joy, and common hopes (Acts 4).

They sensed that the new reality centered in the quality of their fellowship, the warmth and renewing power of their bread breakings, and the life-changing power of their prayers. The apostles selected others to direct their mutual aid program, so they could give their attention to the fellowship meetings, the bread breakings, and prayers (Acts 6:1-6).

The apostles held to this vision of a strong group life and spirit. In founding congregations they tried to realize their Lord's intentions. When Paul told the Ephesian congregation how to stand up against Satan and his dirty tricks, how to work against the wiles of the devil, and how to withstand and to contend against the subtle pressures from the principalities and powers (Ephesians 6:10, 11), what he described was actually a vigorous congregational gathering. In 1 Timothy 3:15, 16 he spoke to the same congregation about conducting themselves as God's household, a family reunion of heaven-bound believers.

The purpose of assembling, Paul said, was to build up one another's strength in union with the living Lord, to be the very body through which the life and strength of Christ flows (Ephesians 1:22, 23), and to experience in their interaction the "strength of his might" (Ephesians 6:10). Early in the letter, in the invocation prayer, Paul asked that the eyes of their understanding might be enlightened to the power available to those who believe—the same power by which God raised Christ from the dead (Ephesians 1:17-20). In my own tradition, the Anabaptists felt that they began to "walk in the resurrection" when they assembled to function as His disciples, to determine His will and proceed to carry it out, even at the price of martyrdom.

The Ephesian congregation was to come together with a sense of awe and expectancy, believing that the same power which burst open a tomb, the same power which swept Christ from a dead body to the throne of the universe, the same power which already has set the risen Christ far above all rule and all authority and power and dominion in all worlds—that this power was to be renewed in them by their group worship.

This power set them above the demons and above the world rulers of this present darkness. I cannot believe that members of the congregation, if feeling oppressed, stole off to seek an exorcist. I can see them coming to the church meeting to stand together against the devil. In Pauline theology, congregational interaction is the place of power, the bearer of healing, the conveyer of grace.

A wide variety of needs were being met in the lives of a wide variety of people as the congregation gathered to build up their strength in God's mighty power. Some persons were seeking intensely for truth, trying to find meaning and wholeness in life, and a world-view within which all things make sense. God's Spirit brooded over the corporate reality to see that each worshiper's need was met. Paul said "having girded your loins with truth" was central in congregational reality.

Other members needed God's righteousness as a breastplate. They needed it to reassure their hearts that God's ways were really right and just. They needed it to rest their anxieties in the loving care of Almighty God. They needed righteousness as God's gift, reassuring them they were after all okay in the eyes of their Maker. They could face their destiny unafraid because of their faith in a righteous God. They had found God's forgiving grace for their own need and felt right with God. This triumphant reality and certainty rendered them practically immune to the "accuser of the brethren." They had not been giving any specific attention to the devil, yet their meeting was exactly the way to stand against him.

Other members possibly felt their need to get ready to tell the good news. In Ephesians 6:15 this is called "having shod your feet with the equipment of the gospel of peace." How should they announce the good news to Demetrius and his guild of silversmiths, whose whole life of luxury was made possible by the demonic, exorcistic worship of Diana? How could they communicate the Jesus movement, a way of life so superior to all Demetrius had ever known, in a way that would impress him with the good news? How could they tell what God was making possible in their fellowship as a glad announcement, the heralding of something infinitely good to every hearer? Such intense questioning and searching for answers was to be going on in the congregation.

And, incidentally, this was the deepest kind of standing together against the principalities and powers.

Still other members in the congregation at Ephesus may have been seeking answers to questions posed by sophisticated neighbors about the meaning of life's sorrows and troubles. Homer's *Iliad* shows Apollo inflicting plague by shooting his darts. Early German folklore called a sudden stitch of pain in the side a "witches shot." Job called his troubles the "arrows of the Almighty" (Job 6:4). Almost every culture has tried to answer the "fiery darts," the way of the suffering of innocents. Only faith is a shield against them. Only a trusting gaze in the face of God as He is seen in Jesus Christ can cope with these "fiery darts of the evil one." Because the sinless Christ suffered, Christian faith need no longer assume that suffering is due to one's sin. Because God brought infinite good out of Christ's suffering, Christian faith can wait for an answer. The story of God's pilgrim people is full of instances in which suffering turned out to be redemptive. I believe that such searching for answers should be constantly going on in our congregational meetings.

The congregational meeting itself is an enactment of God's saving action, His salvation. Not only does the congregation study the ways God saved Noah, rescued Lot, led Abraham, delivered Daniel, changed Peter, and empowered Paul. This congregational meeting is another chapter in holy history. An Abraham in the meeting is being led right here and now. God's saving action is brought up to the present. God is even now saving His people, delivering them, changing them, and empowering them. God's saving action is like a helmet, protecting one's head. One knows that the saving God is still around, alive, in action, and adequate for every need. He is experienced right now in the meeting.

Paul told the Ephesian congregation that a vital part of their standing together against all the powers and wiles of the devil is to be accepting "the sword of the Spirit, which is the word of God" (Ephesians 6:17). A crucial way the gathered congregation accepts salvation, expects and welcomes God's saving action here and now in their very midst, is to accept a fresh word from the living God, proceeding out of the mouth of God to them in their condition. They are to ask God, who spoke to men in the past, to speak with the same creating, life-changing power to them in the present moment and to their present problems.

When God speaks anew to His gathered people, His Word divides their thoughts from their intents, their fuzzy thinking from their clearly formed intentions and determinations, what they believe as a mere idea from what is a life-and-death conviction. God's Word divides thoughts from intents like a two-edged sword.

God's Son declared that we are not really living as long as we subsist on materialism (bread) alone. Real living begins for us when we are in dialogue with our Maker, when we who are addressed by God know what we want to say in response. Our sublimest moments are when we sense that God's Word is coming directly to us, when the thoughts and intents of our hearts are laid bare by that encounter, and when between ourselves and the God of all the earth a "We-Thou" dialogue is going on.

Paul was not only telling the Ephesian congregation that the Scriptures were inspired, as he told their pastor,

Timothy (2 Timothy 3:16). Paul saw the Scriptures as
their way to live-themselves-into their history as God's
people. Through the Scriptures, written for their admonition and learning, they could see how God called, empowered, and preserved a people for centuries past. And
then God's mighty miracle could happen again! God's
living Word could come to them in power. God could
tutor them in His truth. God could rebuke them where
they were drifting into error. God could correct their
faults. God could instruct them in right living. From
such a church meeting and such a dialogue with the living God they could stride forth well able to cope with
the worst that superstitious Ephesus could do to them.
Such a meeting was a tremendous standing against the
devil, even though he had never been mentioned.

A final reality of congregational life is prayer. Christ
wanted the church to keep praying the mutual exorcistic
prayer, "Deliver us from the evil one." He had told the
disciples that prayer precedes the miracles, releases the
power, and brings the victory. Paul believed it too.
"Pray in the Spirit, pray for all the saints, and pray for
me," he said. Prayer protected Job's family from Satan,
and mutual intercessory prayer enables God's family,
the household of God, the church, to stand together
against Satan's wiles.

The early church was led to include exorcism of Satan
into the once-for-all rite and vows of Christian baptism.
Claiming Christ's once-for-all victory on Calvary, and
making vows to be faithful to Christ within His
church—these are the central realities.

It is striking that Paul did not use the athletic model
for the congregational meeting. A game assumes that

the opposition plays by the rules, plays fairly, and therefore predictably within limits. But in meeting the principalities and powers, the forces of evil, preparation must reckon with the fact that the opposition does not play fair. They are not out for a fair test of strength but to destroy. They are not honorable opponents but dishonorable enemies. Paul warned that when the evil day comes and the enemy attacks, we must fight to the end. The church meeting is like the last moments before a bugle call for battle, a time to take up God's armor for the tasks of the coming week (Ephesians 6:13).

Christians engage in an intense refreshing of their faith at every meeting, preparing for their dialogue with the world all week. A lot of their wrestling against entrenched wrong, against principalities and powers, is actually done while they are the church gathered, while they are meeting with the living God, while they are coming to consensus about His will, and while they re-commission one another to serve.

They depart to function as the church scattered, to carry out the implications of what has happened in the church meeting. This is the scriptural ideal.

For Additional Reading and Reference:
Anderson, Philip and Phoebe. *The House Church* (New York: Abingdon Press, 1975).
Bridge, Donald, and Phypers, David. *Spiritual Gifts and the Church* (Downers Grove: Inter-Varsity Press, 1973).
Christenson, Larry. *A Charismatic Approach to Social Action* (Minneapolis: Bethany Fellowship, 1974).
Klassen, William. *The Forgiving Community* (Phil-

adelphia: Westminster Press, 1966).

Kraus, C. Norman. *The Healing Christ* (Scottdale, Pa.: Herald Press, 1972).

Ranaghan, Kevin and Dorothy. *Catholic Pentecostals* (Paramus, N.J.: Paulist Press, 1969).

Robinson, Wayne A. *I Once Spoke in Tongues* (Wheaton: Tyndale, 1973).

Schweizer, Eduard. *Church Order in the New Testament* (London: SCM Press, 1961).

Yoder, John H. *The Politics of Jesus* (Grand Rapids: Eerdmans, 1972).

15
I Don't Accept the Alibi,
"The Devil Made Me Do It"

To my amazement I have discovered that the rituals used by gurus of many non-Christian religions and the rites followed by many Christian exorcists are much alike. They have similar signs by which they detect possession, they claim special power by their linkage to their deity, they take charge and name the opposing demon, they pray and make use of cultic objects (showing the crucifix or mentioning the blood), they issue their word of command, and they engage in preventative follow up.[1]

Within Christ's body, the church, I feel that our ways of helping demonized persons should be characterized by the difference, not the similarities, to pagan exorcism. In chapter 10, I already traced what I believe to be the confrontational teaching method which Paul was commanding Timothy to use as a replacement for the exorcistic rituals with which Timothy's congregation was so familiar. I will not repeat that material. I wish to show here the strengths of the pastoral counseling approach and methods for helping "demonized persons."

First of all, pastoral counseling relies upon congregational realities all the way. Pastoral counseling is done within the congregation, by a servant and equipper (the trained pastor) of the congregation. It is always aligned with everything else that is being experienced in the congregation. It embodies the same gospel which is preached and taught in the congregation. It relies constantly upon the sustaining life and love and power of the groups of the congregation. It seeks to refer the counselee back again, after counseling is terminated, to the congregation's watchful care.

Pastoral counseling, as I attempt to practice it, is an intensified form of the brotherly admonition which is both the duty and privilege of every member. The pastor is himself subject to this brotherly admonition. He seeks and receives it regularly and regards the binding-and-loosing processes of the congregation as among the most important things which are going on.

Christ envisioned for His people, after Pentecost, a new kind of binding and loosing, different from the exorcism rituals of the religions round about. In Matthew 18 He first described the attitudes and inner spirits in which binding and loosing must be attempted. Then He traced the linkage with the church group by which the whole healing, redeeming, restoring of the alienated and estranged person is completed. I see Matthew 18 as setting forth the foundational realities underlying pastoral counseling.

The objective is to win back the sinning, alienated, estranged person. The verb tenses Christ used in Matthew 18:15 give the sense, "If he is hearing you, your gaining of him has already begun." What is that mysterious communication the angry and alienated person is "hear-

ing?" What is in the unverbalized flow of feeling? What
unconditional positive regard is being sensed? What acceptance in advance? What love without limit? What
caring is the counselee "hearing" subverbally?

Christ implied that the counselor who approaches the
sinning, hurting, angry (or possibly even demonized)
person, seeking to bind and loose, should be one in heart
and spirit with the seeking heavenly Father who wills
that not one person be lost (v. 14). He implied, too, that
the counselee must be able to do as Christ did when He
came to save the lost, and as a shepherd does when he
leaves the ninety and nine to go after a lost sheep.

This is hard for any counselor to do. To really leave
the ninety-nine, to go and stand with the lonely and the
lost one, to really exist on his turf, to feel the full weight
of his loneliness, awayness, estrangement, and feeling of
being "out of it," is not easy. Secular counselees seek
this quality out of the well-springs of humanism and
seek to offer empathy. The pastoral counselor shares
this goal but is also aware of the Holy Spirit of the
Father God and His seeking love (vv. 18:10-13). The
more the counselor loves and values his church (his
ninety-nine) the harder it is to really leave them in spirit,
even for a little while, to fully feel with the deviant, the
"lost" one, the demonized one, the outsider, the one
who has sinned.

Christ implied that the hurting, alienated, sinning
person is hearing still more! In Matthew 18:7-9 He implied that the person the counselor is trying to talk to
about his sins, his temptations, or his bondage to his appetites is actually hearing whether the counselor himself
knows the cost of victory over sin. Does the counselor

know, by vigorous self-discipline, the painful cost of deliverance? Has he ever "cut off a hand or foot" (v. 8) of
his own rather than to go on in sin? The counselee is
sensitive of the counselor's lack of self-discipline, his
lack of courage, his fear of pain, his search for an easy
way past the problem. Or he senses the counselor's inner
courage, his integrity, his self-discipline, his honesty,
and his core worth.

Christ probed still deeper as He laid bare inner attitudes of spirit the counselor is tempted to have, and
which the counselee "hears." The counselee senses how
much the counselor really cares about him. Does he care
so much he would rather his voice would be cut off, like
a person being drowned with a millstone around his
neck, rather than to go on and on saying the wrong
things, saying things which his own pride and selfishness
prompts him to say, but which actually harm the
counselee (vv. 18:5, 6)?

The counselor must keep trying, humbly and rev-
erently, to be the servant of God's Spirit, the voice of the
living Christ, gently calling to the deciding counselee. A
study of Christ's own interviews with persons discloses
that He dealt with their hesitations, their hurts, their
reserves, their fears, and their evasions. He invited them
to yield themselves to His call, to allow Christ's
kingdom to replace their own ego plans, and to
experience a new centering in their innermost personality. All these are goals of pastoral counseling.[2]

Christ inferred that the counselee "hears" whether the
counselor himself still has a childlike spirit (vv. 18:1-4).
Has his ordination, his training, the seduction of being
"a great one" in Christ's kingdom made him slow to

respond to the call of Jesus? Is the counselor's own life filled with hang-ups? Has his healthy spontaneity been replaced with inhibitions, taboos, rigidities which slow down his own responses to Jesus Christ? Has the child-likeness gone out of his reflexes and the sense of wonder from his eyes? Is he instead playing to the galleries, deciding first what onlookers will think before he decides to make his own autonomous and spontaneous response to Jesus Christ?

Christ outlined still further the spirit and method of the binding and loosing which was to go on among members of His movement. All of these attitudes the suffering person senses, detects, and "hears" as the counselor initiates, goes to his side, and tries to restore the counselee to full relationships in the fellowship.

Going to the deviant alone shows respect for his feelings, his desire for privacy, his reluctance to air his faults at once before a lot of people (v. 15). If this reverence for the inner secret of the counselee is genuine, the counselee will sense it and hear it.

Switching to group counseling as Christ suggested in Matthew 18:16, inviting one or two witnesses, can also strengthen the situation. The counselor shows he wants his impressions checked out. Truth must be established. If his impressions are wrong, he wants the witnesses to correct him, to represent the sinning brother, to be impartial, fair, honest mediators, seekers for both love and justice. The counseling can be expanded to a larger group, if necessary, that more adequately represents the congregation. The pastor may call in the elders (vv. 16, 17).

Contrary to much Christian and non-Christian exorcism, the pastoral counselor does not take command, take control, take charge, assuming that the deviant is so possessed he has no free will left. Christ clearly insisted that the person's right to say "no" be respected. He must be allowed to take his stand outside of the fellowship if he chooses to do so. He is free to be what he chooses to be. He is helped to clarify his identity. If he chooses to be a "Gentile and tax collector," his choice is respected, his person is respected, and he is not treated as a failure. Christ evidently intended that the deviant be treated just as He treated tax collectors. He invited Himself into the home of Zacchaeus. He called and accepted Matthew. His love never turned away nor fully left them go (v. 17). The pastoral counselor cannot merely dismiss a rebellious counselee and proceed to forget about him or her altogether. That may do for a secular agency, but not for God's people, the church.

The kind of pastoral counseling confrontation described in Matthew 18 is Christ's way to offer the most help to troubled, demonized, or sinning deviants. The binding and loosing done in the attitude and spirit He insisted upon is done simultaneously with heaven. Heaven's binding and loosing parallels this kind of encounter counseling as it is done on earth. Jesus promised, "I'll be there in your midst," when two persons are together in this kind of relatedness, this kind of loving, this kind of setting free, this kind of honesty, and this quality of caring (vv. 18-20). This is the ultimate context of pastoral counseling.

Many exorcists and deliverance ministers feel they are "discerning the spirits" when they name a demon. But "discerning spirits" seems rather to be a sensing of the

Holy Spirit's leading in a meeting, of His gifts in a brother or sister, or of God's prophetic Word for the hour. A church group is discerning the spirits when they are detecting the Spirit-driven consensus which is "seeming good to the Holy Spirit and to us."

The pastoral counselor shares with the counselee the responsibility of discerning what his or her trouble is. Even more, the counselor labors to assist the counselee in coming to self-insight. If the counselee takes the responsibility of searching for the roots of his or her trouble, if the counselee works through to insight, to a solution, to a way of deliverance by small steps of understanding, repentance, and faith—then the counselee is greatly strengthened by the whole experience. His own ego and self-respect grow more than when he is merely told by someone else what his problems are and what the best solution may be.

When the pastoral counselor and counselee together come to an understanding of the underlying sin, lust, demon, attitude, value, or relationship which is causing the trouble, the counselor does not hurry on with a command that the "demon" leave. Rather the counselor works patiently as together they discover the reasons for the difficulty, the growth of the problem, the relationships affected, the cost of needed repentance and restitution, some workable next steps, and a support group to sustain the counselee all the while.

Whereas many services and rituals of exorcism utilize prayers and readings from Scripture, the pastoral counselor has no predetermined formula. He may pray with the counselee, but at a time and in a manner that it can be the counselee's own prayer too. The prayer will grow out of the realities of the counselee's unique situation. Scriptures will not be used because they are prescribed, nor utilized as pressure. Great sensitivity and leading of God's Spirit is needed so that a Scripture is used authentically that applies to the counselee's situation and need, and is not wrested out of context and misapplied. Jesus Christ varied His healing methods to fit every sick person's unique needs. The pastoral counselor tries to do the same.

Because pastoral counseling is committed to congregational realities, seeking to embody the gospel and to apply what Christ taught in Matthew 18, does not lessen the pastoral counselor's concern that he also embody and apply the basic skills of counseling as a profession. These may include setting a clear contract, securing privacy, obtaining a case history, defining terms, exploring emotions, and a careful analysis of various problems. It should include the sensing of deep feelings, of memories uncleansed, of relationships broken, of ideals unmet, of trusts betrayed, and of detour systems being utilized to evade realities.

The pastoral counselor values highly the skills which help to increase the effectiveness of listening love. He will seek to intervene strategically to know when to be supportive, probing, understanding, and confronting. He will use summaries skillfully. He will reflect back inconsistencies. He will speak the truth in love. He will refuse to take responsibility or to "play God."

The pastoral counselor must refuse any "bag of tricks" approach, with a predetermined set of techniques to be used in every case. He may or may not use silence, or restatement, or interpretation, or explanation, depending on whether they are helpful to the particular counselee.

The pastoral counselor dare not become captive to any school of counseling. At times he may only listen, empathize, reflect back, clarify, and support. For other needs he may seize the "teachable moment" and seem almost to urge, to confront, or to advise.

Some responses which ought never occur in the ministry of a pastoral counselor include threat, criticism, ridicule, command, scolding, moralizing, or rejection.

Although the pastoral counselor is often called upon to do preaching, exposition of Scriptures, teaching, and proclamation of the good news, he will be wise to discipline himself to loving listening, to drawing out, to a mastery of the nondirective styles as well.

For Additional Reading and Reference:

Adams, Jay E. *Competent to Counsel* (Grand Rapids: Baker Book House, 1970).

Benjamin, Alfred D. *The Helping Interview* (Boston: Houghton Mifflin, 1969).

Clinebell, Howard J., Jr. *Basic Types of Pastoral Counseling* (New York: Abingdon Press, 1966).

Colston, Lowell G. *Judgment in Pastoral Counseling* (New York: Abingdon Press, 1969).

Ford, Peter S. *The Healing Trinity* (New York: Harper & Row, 1971).

Jeschke, Marlin. *Discipling the Brother* (Scottdale, Pa.: Herald Press, 1972).

Leslie, Robert. *Jesus and Logotherapy* (New York: Abingdon Press, 1965).

May, Rollo. *The Art of Counseling* (New York: Abingdon Press, 1967).

Nouwen, Henri. *The Wounded Healer: Ministry in Contemporary Society* (New York: Doubleday, 1972).

Oates, Wayne E. *Pastoral Counseling* (Philadelphia: Westminster Press, 1974).

Smith, Nancy C. *Journey Out of Nowhere* (Waco: Word, 1973).

Part II

Additional Observations

1

Questions Frequently Asked

1. *Isn't the devil stronger than we are? If so, can't he "make us do it?"*

It is true that the Bible pictures Satan as more powerful than man. One New Testament scholar I know has concluded that the devil is above man, and more powerful than human beings; but he sees Satan's imps, the demons, as being below human beings, and of lesser power. I can find little exegetical evidence myself for this precise heirarchical rating.

It is likely not possible to rate nonhuman personages, whoever they are, in a nicely graded ascending order of power and strength. There is some biblical warrant to conclude that Satan is more powerful than man, but only in man's unaided human strength.

The reason "the devil cannot make me do it" is because my God is all powerful, I have committed my life completely into His care, and He has set limits to what Satan can do. If I understand scriptural teachings rightly, Satan must have both God's and my permission before he can hurt me. God's Holy Spirit dwells within me and possesses me. The church is His body, renewed by life and impulses from Christ, the Head, and I am a part of that body. Christ's victory over Satan, at Calvary and on Easter morning, was so decisive and so all-inclusive that Satan's head gets crushed under my feet as I simply go on seeking to be wise as to what is good and innocent and as to what is evil (Romans 16:20). I am not at Satan's mercy.

2. *Are troubled, demonized people really helped by exorcism?*

Yes, I think some of them are. Scientific follow-up studies of the famous healing shrine at Lourdes reveal that less than one percent are really healed in a way that is medically verifiable. But that tiny percentage keeps Lourdes going. I have a feeling that something like this is the case in modern exorcism.

There is a tremendous certainty which some Christians feel after they have either been delivered or have conducted a few exorcisms. Their confidence seems so absolute and their formula for helping so extremely simple. A friend of mine told me that he had done all he could as a devout Christian therapist for more than two years of intense sessions in his effort to help a deteriorating patient. Then some exorcists got hold of her, named her demons, and cast them out. Now his former patient is again bright-eyed, intelligent looking, mothering her family, and feverishly going out to help cast demons out of other persons. My therapist friend is puzzled. There is still a certain hysterical and compulsive quality about the "healed" woman's life. Few mental health specialists would consider her as "well" or stabilized, but at least she has found a style of coping for the present.

Paul said he was confident that preaching the gospel would bring blessing to hearers, even though some who preached it did so because they wanted to get Paul into greater trouble. He still believed God would bless people.

I, too, believe that God is eager to bless and to set free. It is entirely possible that He will sometimes bless persons through exorcism, even though He would have preferred another way of pastoral care. I cannot deny that some people are being helped, and for this I am glad.

3. *Is there agreement among the exorcists regarding haunted houses?*

I am puzzled how intolerant my exorcist friends (and I do have quite a few of them) are of one another on this issue. One of them gladly goes out when called upon to name demons and cast them out of distressed persons. Another exorcist also casts demons out of haunted houses. But my first exorcist friend denounces this activity vehemently as "superstition." Each exorcist seems to be a law unto himself.

4. *What do exorcists include among occult activities to be avoided?*

Deliverance ministers differ radically regarding "occult activities" which Christians must avoid. Some include water witching (hunting for underground water by the use of a peach twig) as fully occult, as bad as Ouija boards of Satan worship. Others think it is a neutral or purely "human" phenomena. One of my exorcist friends sincerely believes that the blighting effects of Amish

ancestors who practiced magical powwowing may cause
demon possession even to the fourth generation of their
children. Others doubt this completely, as I also do.

All the exorcists I have heard or read agree that
activities known to be related to Satan worship or idol
worship must be put away and destroyed. To this I
agree.

I am distressed by the insistence of some exorcists that
persons' lives are blighted if they ever played with
certain "magical stuff" even in childish innocence. I feel
this contradicts God's sovereign grace as I trust it.

5. *Do many pastors utilize exorcism as part of the regular
pastoral care of their members?*

Apparently most pastors who utilize exorcisms perform these ministries away from home, at retreats, in
specialized prayer and praise meetings. One pastor told
me recently that he cast the demon of masturbation
from a middle-aged Christian man of his congregation,
but that he seldom performed exorcisms in his midweek
prayer meeting. Another pastor came to me for help because his members "vomited so much" when he expelled
their demons. I was not surprised to learn that, in less
than a year, he had left this pastorate!

I don't want to leave the impression that no pastors
combine exorcisms with the ongoing pastoral care of
their own congregations. Knowing my feelings about
exorcisms as a method of pastoral care, those who are
doing so might be reluctant to tell me. I simply do not
know how much "naming of demons" pastors are doing.

I tried, but was unable to help an immigrant from

Mexico who was sure an evil spell had been put upon her by a jealous in-law. One of the pastors worked with me, using the teaching-repentance-and-faith approach: We met with her in her home.

An assistant pastor tried exorcism and likewise was unable to help. Relief from her fears and oppression came later on, slowly, as the accepting love of the congregation did its work in her life, the pastoral preaching bore its fruit, and she matured in her Christian life.

6. *Do exorcists cast demons from children?*

I find my exorcist friends at opposite poles on whether to cast demons out of children. One fervent couple in Arizona was doing so with their own and other infants. An equally sincere couple, who attended lectures I gave in Pennsylvania, felt led to quit the practice for anyone not an adult.

There is a great deal of secrecy about exorcism and the naming and casting out of demons. Persons who are naming demons in children may not be talking about it.

I have felt strong disapproval in most of my lecture-discussions whenever the matter of exorcizing demons from children was mentioned. I strongly disapprove of the practice.

7. *Do missionary administrators urge exorcisms?*

At one three-day study conference in which I shared, I heard several medical missionary doctors and educators urge exorcism as a necessary part of missionary ministry. But almost always when I spoke to the missionary in private, he saw exorcism as being "for them" or necessary for "the animistic field." But not once can I

recall that the missionary himself either performed it for
others or asked for it to help him in times of his own
temptation. Yet missionaries serving among all forms of
voodoo and animistic religions have attended my lectures at various places.

I keep getting mixed messages also from professors of
several schools of missions, and the reports from various
mission fields do not agree. I received strong endorse-
ment of my lectures in writing from several administra-
tors of overseas missions, but I cannot at all claim to be
speaking for missiologists.

8. *Is exorcism used with persons in the back wards of
   mental hospitals where so many feel that they are
   demon possessed?*

No, it is not used in mental hospitals to my
knowledge. Some people refer to the back wards of
mental hospitals as the place to which "possessed"
persons are heading if their demons are not cast out. But
over the past twelve years I have served three different
times, for eleven weeks each, as either chaplain or supervisor of chaplains, in three different mental hospitals. I
have counseled a great many persons who felt they were
"possessed." I supervised a pastor who had been exorcising demons from the members of nearby parishes,
utilizing the service from the Order of St. Luke, the Physician. But when he actually served back ward persons
day after day as chaplain, he never once mentioned the
exorcism service to them.

9. *What do Christian psychiatrists say about exorcism?*
   I don't know of thorough research on this question. I

can report that some of the most devout Christians I have ever worked with ("Bible believing and born again," as many of my evangelical friends would be glad to know) have been among the psychiatrists I have conferred with about "possessed" patients and about exorcism as a way of helping them. But so far not one of these seven or eight devout psychiatrists has ever considered using exorcism rituals to help. One psychiatrist, who regularly prays with his deeply-disturbed patients, told me that he has often observed patients from whom demons have been cast by Christian exorcists. They seem to be helped for a while, perhaps three weeks, and then are worse off than before.

Dr. R. Kenneth McAll, consultant psychiatrist of Lyndhurst, Hants, England, cites ten representative cases of exorcism in which he shared, from among 280 of which he has records. He warns that many patients suffer "from treatable diseases for whom a service such as an exorcism might have detrimental effect."[1]

In his careful descriptions of "the possession syndrome," Dr. McAll seldom if ever calls the possessing entity a "demon." In one case study it was a lesbian friend's influence; in another a dead mother who had been extremely domineering; in another "an occult group"; and in still others an occult-practicing ancestor, a spiritualist healer, a medium, a fortune-teller, and a mother who dabbled in witchcraft.

Because of his medical training, he was able to diagnose the real problem of a woman who was sure she was demon possessed because she had "little demons dancing before her eyes." He treated her for her pernicious anemia and the dancing spots ceased. He demonstrated his pastoral concern by probing her guilts until he found she had stolen a bishop's crozier. When she returned this stolen item, Dr. McAll reports, "she was fully restored to health." This, in my mind, represents a helpful naming of the real demon.

I have conferred at great length with Dr. McAll myself, and am astounded at his psychiatric sophistication combined with a faith in the power of prayer which is childlike in its simplicity. He thinks that even a child has the right to say, "In the name of Christ, Satan, get behind me."

10. *Should we expect to utilize exorcism among Christians newly converted from animism?*

I understand those who urge the use of exorcism among people recently converted from animism. But in actual practice I have found exorcism flourishing most among college and university students in America and among middle-class whites. I encountered little exorcism during the years I served in East Africa. Blacks and Spanish-American Christians in younger churches in North America also seem to avoid exorcism. They regard it as akin to a superstitious past they have left behind.

A brilliant and deeply Christian middle-class white college professor was casting demons from troubled students in a college the week before I was scheduled to come there for a series of spiritual renewal services. One demon he cast out said it was going to kill a person who was coming to the campus on Monday. It was obvious to all the students that I was that person! Many students insisted upon laying hands upon me in prayer for my protection that week. A sense of expectancy and near-fear brooded in many minds. I felt it keenly.

The student from whom the demon had been cast came in near hysteria to see me. She tore a cactus plant in half and asked me to plant the one half in a pot in my house while she planted the other half in a pot on her dorm windowsill. She said it would be "a tribute of life between us that my demon will not kill you." I don't know how her half is coming, but my half slowly died after two years of struggle to survive! (I'm glad I don't tend to be superstitious!)

The therapist in a church-related psychiatric center who had treated this girl in sustained, intensive therapy before she came to college, learned that the college prof had exorcized demons from her. He called to protest vehemently against such treatment of a convalescing patient. My own years of experience as a counselor and therapist lead me to feel that this girl's recovery was delayed and not helped by the deliverance ministries of the well-meaning college professor. I felt that my ministry of preaching and counseling on the campus was hindered and not helped.

Christian leaders who have grown up in an animistic country and who understand their culture in its depth should lead out in applying biblical teachings to their congregations. I would not presume to say how Africans should conduct healing services in their churches.

11. *From what theological background do the modern deliverance ministers come?*

In my experience the "deliverance ministry" appears with equal fervency and frequency among almost all kinds of theological traditions. Having taught in graduate level theology for more than two decades, I tend to expect some things to appear among fundamentalists, other things among liberals, still others among charismatics, biblical realists, the neoorthodox, sacramentalists, religious commune advocates, and main-line evangelicals. But none of the usual categories are useful in studying the exorcism movement. "Deliverance ministers" come from all parts of the spectrum, and among persons who have almost nothing else in common. All the exorcists I know personally are warmly evangelical.

I have noticed almost no exorcists arising from among biblical scholars and Bible instructors in colleges or seminaries. I do know of one Old Testament scholar who was dismissed by his fundamentalist school when he became active in exorcism. I have been getting the most guidance precisely from my biblical studies, although readings in psychology, in psychology of religion, pastoral care, anthropology, and missions have been useful in a secondary way.

12. *From what walks of life do exorcists come?*

Among my friends who are active in exorcism are a salesman, a schoolteacher, a welder, a professor of sociology, two teachers of evangelism, a mission administrator, and four pastors. I have met many more whose background I did not learn. Almost all of them utilize their Bibles to support their deliverance ministry, but largely by assembling proof texts. I know of no persons who have worked out a theological rationale for their practice.

Roman Catholic "deliverance ministers" tend to include prayers to the virgin, incense, use of the crucifix, and holy water as part of their service of deliverance. Most of the Protestant exorcists I know would be strongly opposed to such practices. Ecumenical fellowship appears to be acceptable when exorcism is the focus for discussion, but in actuality most exorcists have their own special rituals.

13. *Do those who expect to identify demons in one another also stress the presence and influence of good, guardian angels?*

Since the biblical record reports twice as many angel incidents as demon incidents among God's people, one would expect this to be true today too. God's people today certainly believe that God is able and willing to send forth ministering spirits to those who are heirs of salvation (Hebrews 1:14).

H. A. Turner's study of African independent groups of believers reveals that they do stress very much the presence of guardian angels. I have scanned a number of volumes reporting on the African independent churches and find only scant mention of exorcism and the naming of demons. I personally interviewed thirty-five of their leaders in East Africa and not one of them mentioned any conflict with demons.

I wish that Western Christians, currently so interested in demons, could learn a lesson from African Christians. Wouldn't it be an amazingly wholesome way of Christian victory if believers could say, as Christ did, that they can call upon twelve legions of angels if needed (Matthew 26:53).

14. *If one believes in miracles at all, isn't it natural to ex-*
pect the drastic miracle of exorcism?

I personally know of one exorcist who returned to a
belief in miracles after he viewed an exorcism. For my
part, I've never ceased believing in miracles and don't
find exorcism a necessary aid in this matter. I am as
much impressed, and even excited, about God's many
quiet miracles as by the few spectacular ones He chooses
to perform. The quiet miracle of the new birth, of the
formation of a human eye in the womb of a mother, and
the healing of spirit which Christian reconciliation
brings—these continue to astound me. I find myself looking ever more alertly for the miracles which accompany
repentance and faith. I'm glad for the "natural laws"
God has set in motion. I find His miracles within all of
His ways, and not particularly in an event which seems
to go against or interrupt one of nature's laws. To me it
seems easier to "explain" an exorcism psychologically
and psychiatrically than it is to explain the quiet miracle
of repentance and faith which happens so mysteriously.

The greatest miracles of the Christian faith are still the
quiet ones—the incarnation with the quiet coming of
God's life into a human being, the convicting of sin by
the Holy Spirit, or the salvation which happens as God's
love proves itself again to be stronger than sin and
death. Christ's resurrection and our rising to newness of
life are quiet miracles. Changes into Christ's likeness
often come by quiet miracles of grace. Most answers to
prayer come as quiet miracles. The miracle of wholeness
which enables the person to say, "Get thee behind me,
Satan!" is a quiet miracle. The gracious workings of the
Holy Spirit and the fruit of love, joy, peace, long-suffer-

ing, gentleness, goodness, faith, temperance, and meekness are usually quiet miracles of God's love and power.

15. *You base your position upon a study of the epistles. Upon what passages do the exorcists and deliverance ministers base their practice of exorcism?*

Kurt Koch, who is probably the most prolific writer on exorcism, bases his case strongly upon the passage in Mark 5:1-20. He builds his ritual, point by point, from the case of the demoniac whose legion of demons was sent into the swine. All other exorcists imply that we are to follow in Christ's steps. If He and the apostles cast out demons, and if Christ's Great Commission gives us the authority to do so, we should continue this practice to the end of time. It's just that simple in many minds.

I feel that Christ's exorcisms were signs of His kingdom's inbreaking, and that the church need not struggle to duplicate them any more than His stilling of the storm, raising of Lazarus, or turning the water into wine. After the Holy Spirit and the inspired writings were given to the Jesus movement, the apostles (in writing through their epistles) turned rather to the quiet miracles of preaching, teaching, healing, praying, laying on of hands, coming to Spirit-led consensus, and finding a faith which could endure martyrdom.

Thus far I have neither read nor met an exorcist who has studied all of the mentions of Satan or the devil in both the prophetic writings and the epistles and who has tried to draw out the inferences of these writings for exorcism.

I firmly believe that many of the deliverance ministers and exorcists who practice the naming of demons look to the Scriptures for guidance just as sincerely as I try to do. For this reason I share my findings and conclusions, believing that such persons will seek to prove all things and hold fast to that which is good (1 Thessalonians 5:21).

16. *Do you find aversion to the subjects of Satan, exorcism, and how to find victory over the evil one?*

Yes, I do, and I think I understand why so many devout Christians seem determined to avoid any discussion at all of the pros or cons of exorcism. In contrast to the few who are openly fascinated with the subject, and the many who secretly read the best sellers which deal with it, the great majority say they hope the problem will just go away. Repeatedly, sincere friends have hinted that I should write my book quickly and get back again to crucial issues. I confess that I do want to give my testimony regarding the way of victory over Satan, and then move on to issues still more central in the gospel.

Some feel even more strongly. They feel that it is not only wasted time to talk about the devil and how to have victory over him. They suggest that Satan, the father of lies, is so totally perverted that attention of any kind to him is really the falling down to worship him which he seeks. They see even a study of victory over the devil as dangerous, useless, and a mistake. For them the true victory over the devil comes by concentrating upon Jesus Christ and ignoring Satan altogether.

Responses at a Roman Catholic college where I gave a series of lectures were strongest in insisting that a place be left for much that is neither demonic nor angelic, neither a devil nor God's Holy Spirit at work, but a third category—merely human. Some at this college insisted that parapsychology, poltergeist phenomena, levitation, Ouija boards, pendulums, and the like, be regarded as merely human, and not necessarily demonic.

17. *Doesn't Christian education usually reduce exorcism?*

Yes, the evidence from history seems to show that Christianity usually drives out exorcism. The badly degenerate and superstitious Catholicism of the Middle Ages abounded with exorcism, but reformation and renewal reduced it.

Oesterreich summarizes 378 pages of discussion about possession and exorcisms with the statement, "Manifestations of possession are everywhere in regression among primitive peoples in places where the Christian missions have struck deep root."[2] The church of England tried to outlaw exorcism rituals in 1603.

18. *Is it true that exorcism tends to be divisive in the church?*

Yes, it is. People who have been experiencing charismatic renewal and revival divide vehemently over the matter of exorcism! It is true that tongues-speaking is attributed to filling by the Holy Spirit, but it is also sometimes listed as a sign of demon possession.

I have been appalled to discover that equally-sincere charismatics, whose experience and teaching is almost identical on nearly every other aspect of the charismatic life, can anathematize, outlaw, turn against, and denounce one another simply because the one favors performing exorcisms and the other does not. I wish that this was only the rare exception, but I am afraid it is not. Exorcism may well be one of the most divisive issues of our time.

One of the most heartbreaking stories I have ever heard of separation, wrecked friendship, rejection, repudiation, anger, and refusal of all attempts of reconciliation was told to me by a Christian lady, a friend of mine who speaks in tongues, sings in tongues, and enjoys charismatic worship. She told of a dear friend of many years who shared her deepest experiences of charismatic worship, who then went on to a belief in the naming and casting out of demons. As an exorcist, she discerned a demon in my friend and wanted to cast it out. My friend refused and insisted that she had no demon within her and was rejoicing in Jesus every day. My friend asked that any lack of holy living be pointed out to her so that she could confess it and repent from it. Instead the former friend (now turned exorcist or deliverance minister) told her to get out, leave the city at once, and never to cross her path again.

19. *Did Paul use exorcism to deal with carnality, lusts of the flesh, worldliness, and immaturity?*
    The answer to this is no. The Corinthian congregation was Paul's "swinger" group, with wide extremes. Because the Corinthian congregation had within it both spiritually gifted members and members with devilish carnality and sin, one might expect that exorcisms would be described frequently. A careful study reveals none at all.

Although the Jews there were asking for miraculous

proofs, which exorcism might have provided, none occurred. Instead Paul relied, as always, upon proclaiming
Christ's victory (1 Corinthians 2:4).

He stressed, not the demons that dwelt in the carnal
and the sinning, but the Holy Spirit indwelling, and the
strivings of God's Spirit against fleshly lusts (1 Corinthians 3:16).

When the incestuous brother had to be dealt with,
Paul carefully omitted instructions to exorcize the
demon out of the brother. He rather invoked the name
of Jesus to expel the brother from the fellowship.

The nearest to exorcism Paul came was "fencing the
table," insisting that the Lord's Supper be reserved for
those who were calling Christ Lord, and who gave no
practical reality to the devils so abundant in the idola-
trous culture around them (1 Corinthians 10:15-22).

Paul believed Christ had reduced to impotence the
demons by His victory on Calvary's cross and by His
triumphant resurrection, and that Christ will abolish
entirely all rule, power, and enemy opposition in the
end, when even death is conquered (1 Corinthians
15:20).

Paul might have been contrasting his own ministry of
preaching, exhorting, confronting, warning, pleading,
praying, visiting, and the like with that of the exorcists
and their rituals when he said, "We use no hocus pocus,
no clever tricks" (2 Corinthians 4:1, *Weymouth*).

Paul confronted, not the demon after he has discerned
and named him, but the believer. He demanded whether
there be harmony between Christ and the devil and what
common ground the temple of God has with idols
(2 Corinthians 6:16). He said that believers were

responsible, even as was Eve, if they listened to the tempter (2 Corinthians 11:2-5).

Instead of looking for the devil in every member, so as to name it and cast it out, Paul laid bare the real masquerading of Satan as an "angel of light" in false teachers. He did not confront these false teachers face to face, but promised they would get their deserts one day (2 Corinthians 11:15).

20. *What about the "levels" of demonism, from oppression, obsession, infestation, to possession?*

Deliverance ministers usually say that if the devil is on the outside of a person, he can merely harass or oppress, but if he gets inside he can possess the person. These terms have emerged recently, out of the experiences of the exorcists. They lack firm exegetical foundation in Scriptures, and I have not found my Christian psychiatrist friends able to identify these differences clinically.

Obviously, people experience different degrees of wretchedness and are able to summon differing amounts of freedom and willpower to cope with their situation. Wise counselors and therapists should observe these variables in each person's situation.

The February 10, 1974, issue of *Sunday Visitor* (Roman Catholic) defined "obsession" as the evil spirit's hostile action from without and "possession" as a demon entering a body to control its faculties.

Since the terms lack both biblical and clinical-psychiatric precision, I prefer not to use them. Labels quickly turn to libels. I have seen too many people harmed by having psychiatric labels (paranoid, schizophrenic, and the like) attached to them. I fear persons are likely to be hurt more than helped by having their problem named as a demon, or their problem's seriousness rated by the oppression-possession terminology.

Some insist that "dermatographia" (warnings written on the victim's skin by blotches and stigmata) are a sure sign of possession. But stigmata have also been seen as signs of saintly holiness and devotion. So this evidence is not conclusive.

A phenomena labeled "mythomania" (the inevitable tendency of a weird story to grow more and more weird in the retelling), is also reported by investigators.

21. *Isn't the ability to cast out demons one of the signs that should keep following us if we believe ? Isn't this the promise of Mark 16:17?*

I think God can grant Apostle Paul the power to exorcise the demon from a slave girl or to pick up a serpent without being bitten. Obviously, God can continue to give His faithful servants the power to cope, until the ends of time and to the ends of the earth, with all they meet as they seek to evangelize the world.

But it is one thing for Paul to be preserved from snakebite when he meets it, unsought, on an evangelistic mission. It is an entirely different thing to emphasize snake handling, and to start a church based upon this ability.

In like manner God still honored exorcisms when they were forced upon Paul, but it is clear in all his epistles that he turned away from their use. Even where exorcism through the use of his hankies erupted at Ephesus, he ignored it completely.

The earliest churches did not have the last verses of

Mark in their manuscripts. These verses were added to later manuscripts. Still more exorcism stories appear in the noncanonical books. These books the church felt led to exclude from the canon altogether.

I think our practice should be guided by the recurring refrains of all of the apostles in all of the epistles. Some snake handling cults claim their authority by appealing to the last verses of Mark 16, but this is a risky way to decide church practice!

22. *What is the meaning of Satan being bound during the millennium?*

The dispensationalist theory of prophetic interpretation foresees a 1,000-year reign of Jesus Christ from King David's throne in Jerusalem during which time Satan will be bound in the bottomless pit. They base this upon a literal interpretation of Revelation 20:1-3. Then after the 1,000 years, Satan is loosed and judged and cast into the lake of fire and brimstone (Revelation 20:7-10).

One of the most vivid and popular presentations of this view is Hal Lindsey's *There's a New World Coming.* The table of contents reveals that he elaborates upon the "Demonic Locusts," the "Covenant with Antichrist," the "Satanic Xmas," "The Great Red Dragon," "Satan Is a Snake," "Antichrist's Pal, the False Prophet," "A Closer Look at the Beast," "Antichrist and the Prophet Judged," "Why Bind Satan?" and "Satan Unbound and Judged."

Dispensationalists insist that Satan appears under many differing personalities and with vastly differing freedom in differing dispensations. But their deeper views of God's sovereignty over Satan, of Christ's victory over him, and of his ultimate defeat are similar to those of other evangelical Christians. Dispensationalists tend to see the church as subordinate in God's plan, merely occupying the parenthesis while Israel is in unbelief. For this reason they may not stress the miraculous power inherent in the church, in her prayers, her sacraments, and her consensus. Yet it is precisely the power of congregational life and reality which is the strongest resource a believer has against Satan. (See chapter 14 of this book.)

23. *Is the devil a person?*

Even though personal pronouns are used to refer to Satan—and such personal attributes as speech, the ability to scheme, to dialogue, to oppose, to remember, to be proud, to accept limits, to accuse, to seduce, to appraise values, and to probe meanings are all assigned to him—yet many Christian thinkers hesitate to call the devil a "person" in the same sense that God is a person. There is too great a gulf between God and Satan to use one term to describe them both.

Is a being which does not possess the image of God, nor His Holy Spirit, who cannot love normally, nor repent, nor create, nor commune with God worshipfully, nor give and receive forgiveness still be said to be a person in the fullest sense of the term?

It may be that the Genesis writer was profoundly correct in calling Satan a "subtle beast." He certainly lacks the highest, noblest, and most sacred aspects of personhood. One devout Bible scholar insists that if we use the word "person" for such a creature as Satan, then God must be "supra-person."

24. *In addition to a scripturally-based study, what light might "psychology of religion" offer?*

In this book I have tried to reflect upon the scriptural teachings as the supreme source of truth about man's relation to the spirit world. However, we need not deny the objective reality of Satan at all, or of scriptural teachings about Satan, if we turn also to psychology and the subjective view of man's functioning. This would require another book, but it is one which should be written.

The clinical details about the total social, physical, and mental situation of the demonized persons Christ healed are not adequate to do differential diagnosis. We cannot know what a battery of tests at a Menninger clinic would have revealed about the maniac of Gadora with a thousand demons.

I can venture a few observations from the "psychology of religion" approach. Each school of psychology would notice a particular aspect of the possessed man's experience.

The *ego psychologists* would observe that the sufferer's ego was still intact enough that he could examine and reflect upon the thousand alien forces which beset him. His ego identity was strong enough that he could recognize Jesus as the Son of the Most High God (Luke 8:28). He could admit his own fragmented condition, the portion which was "me" and the portion which was "not me." He could admit that he was clearer about who Jesus was than about who he himself really was. He possessed considerable ego strength, in spite of the fact that his inner life was chaotic.

The *behaviorists* would notice the long conditioning of

rejection: "he was kept under guard" (Luke 8:29); "for a long time he had worn no clothes" (v. 27); "he lived not in a house" (v. 27); "no one could bind him any more" (Mark 5:3); "no one had the strength to subdue him" (v. 4); and he "was driven . . . into the desert" (Luke 8:29). They would observe how his defenses went down as Christ talked with him, allowed him to sit at His feet, to wear clothes again, to feel in his right mind again, and then to go and tell how much God in His mercy had done for him.

The *relationship and responsibility therapists* would observe the way Christ moved past all barriers to enter relationship with the lonely, alienated person. Christ went to the unclean Gentile country, to the unclean tombs, to be with the unclean man with the unclean spirit. He made Himself vulnerable to rejection and being asked to leave the country.

He held the man responsible to name himself, rather than to accept all the labels, stereotypes, and insults others heaped upon him. He held him responsible to come and sit at His feet, to clothe himself, and to declare his healing to his townsmen. He held him responsible to call the people "friends" who had scorned, bound, rejected, hurt, and segregated him. Jesus said, "Go home to your friends." He held him responsible to forgive his tormentors, outgrow his past, restructure his life's relationships, and to take his place courageously with the Jesus movement. He "began to proclaim . . . how much Jesus had done for him; and all men marveled," is the way Mark closes the story (5:20).

In commenting upon all of the New Testament reportings of demons and exorcism (and not merely upon the not-quite-typical case of the Gadarene demoniac) a number of psychologists of religion are urging that persons must incorporate their demon's attacks into a new and integrated personality structure. Job must take into his very life the painful realities of the death of his children and the loss of all he owned when Satan attacked him. Paul must take into his self-image the thorn in the flesh which came as a messenger of Satan to buffet him. Peter must include his self-image the reality that, when Satan sifts as wheat, he too is a denier of Christ and has the awful potential to be a betrayer right in his very nature. Judas must humbly admit that one side of himself values thirty pieces of silver more than Christ.

Carl Jung, the mighty successor and eclipser of Freud as a psychological interpreter of man's depths, has been a leader in the point of view outlined above. Morton Kelsey, a leading Jungian-oriented theologian, educator, and psychologist of religion, is currently exploring this theme in a number of writings and lectures. William Glasser is stressing "responsibility therapy," and Paul A. Hauck "rational-emotive therapy," both of which honor the person's free will and ability to take responsibility for one's total self and situation.

2
*Pastoral Care of Demonized Persons**

1. *Pastoral care should serve the whole person in his whole situation.* Usually the people of the congregation are drawn from a similar culture. They understand one another's world-view. They can bear one another's burdens because they share so many common meanings.

At its truest and deepest level, pastoral care is the total caring love which the entire Spirit-bearing congregation provides for one another. Their help of a "demonized" member will be truer and more total because they also know his secret fears, his intuitive taboos, his sources of hope and strength, his feelings about the spirit which animates nature, his ways of coping with death and destiny, and his notion regarding the ways in which ancestral spirits might relate to God's Holy Spirit or to a demonic, evil spirit.

Unfortunately, many of the scholarly consultations and writings about demonized persons and how to help them have come from "expatriates," missionaries and

---

*A similar treatment of the material in this chapter was released by Mennonite Board of Missions, Elkhart, Indiana, in 1976 as a pamphlet.

researchers groping their way across vast gulfs of culture. Thus far the semantic confusions have far outrun the agreements, in spite of good intentions, reverent approach, hard work, and a solid empirical base. Scholars do seem to agree that "demonized" is the most accurate modern term for "possession by a demon."

Within each culture, if both pastor and people are from the same or at least similar cultures, and if the pastor is well trained in the heritage of biblical revelation and the lessons of church history, hopefully, the wisdom God's Spirit ever gives to His believing people as they seek to be faithful and to claim their rightful victory will be given to the congregation. After all, the pastor is primarily the equipper or enabler of God's ministering people so that they may minister most powerfully to one another and to the world. God's people themselves really provide the pastoral care.

The wisdom which may come as pastoral caring love serves demonized people and should be added to that which God is giving through other studies. The pastor may refer persons to other specialists and they to him.[1]

2. *Pastoral care grows out of intensive listening and long-term, loving involvement with the demonized person.* The caring congregation is all too keenly aware that deep hurt plagues some people through the influences of their families, community, and personal trauma.

The pastor will join his congregation in listening deeply to the erupting fears of the neighbors and friends they need to evangelize. He will try to understand the hunger for the transcendent and the eternal which might lie beneath the drug trips, the oriental gurus, the astrology columns in the papers, the cultic religions, the devil-theme in novels, the rise of charismatic deliverance ministers, the Jesus freaks, the witches and witch hunts, the occult paraphenalia, the seances, and the interest of sober men of science in parapsychology. Members of the congregation also are affected by these same fears.[2]

From his immersion in the wisdom of the Bible and church history, the pastor will call his people away from fascination with the occult, to a scripturally informed search for a way to understand and to serve. Christian faith does have something very profound to say to the fears of man, his sins, and all that destroys his wholeness.

The pastor who has studied his Bible in its wholeness and total sweep will notice that, although exorcism and demonism was intense in Egypt when God called out His people Israel, it declined rapidly through the Mosaic, psalms, and Prophetic influence because monotheism was so high. He will observe also that, although exorcism and demonism had peaked again when God's Son came for "Exodus No. 2," the apostles in their epistles to the church led God's people away from exorcism as vigorously as the prophets had earlier led Israel away from it. The biblically taught pastor helps his congregation to claim their place again as the people of a God who is fully omnipotent.[3]

The pastor might well heed the first instruction the Roman Catholic Church gives to a priest who may function as an exorcist, "Don't believe too readily that anyone is possessed of a demon." Since Satan is totally a liar, profound disbelief is an appropriate approach. Since God's Son came to destroy the works of the devil, the pastor will approach the problem with a patient attitude and will not be swayed by sensational movies or religious best-sellers.

3. *Wise congregational leaders will avail themselves of (and share with their people) some of the things cultural analysts are finding in their patient looking and listening-in on all the world's culture.*[4]

Behind the puzzling patterns of cultic control, exorcism, religious ritual, or taboo, they will see the attempts of a community to strengthen their common understanding of evil and inner cohesion against it. They will notice how persons of all cultures try to cope with the divine power beyond themselves, the time beyond their death, the dead relatives beyond their reach, and the forces that seem to destroy them. They will ponder the ways religions and cults use to sharpen the group's awareness of right and wrong behavior, how to deal with the deviant, and how to get him or her reinstated. They will observe the stress situations which seem to trigger periodic flare-ups of the demonic, and the "underdog" group from which the most of the "demonized" seem to come.[5]

The pastoral care approach is strongest at precisely these points—strengthening God's people through Word and sacrament, strengthening community through the renewal of covenants, commitments to holy living, mutual confession and intercessory prayer, and through grace received from Jesus Christ.

All of these will be part of the reflections of the pastor and his team of congregational leaders as they seek to serve demonized and the suffering within their group and among their neighbors. The common insights about "the demonized" in other cultures will first be refracted, repolarized, and rethought in terms of the gospel, the Christian world-view, and the realities of a Spirit-filled, Spirit-led congregation. Just as the Apostle Paul welcomed the medical doctor, Luke, as a strong member of the pastoral team, so Christian psychiatrists should serve on today's pastoral team.

God's Spirit and power among His people is able to do much more than they can fully understand, but that does not absolve God's people from the obligation to be sober, thoughtful, and vigilant. Magic and superstition are always wrong.

4. The pastor and his team of leaders instinctively "take a running start" in biblical or holy history before they take action about a problem in demonism in the congregation or community. They see their congregation's life as the "now-testament," which God's Spirit is writing. They see their people in solid and unbroken continuity with the people of the Exodus, psalms, prophets, Gospels, Acts, and Epistles. Only a thorough mastery of the tested wisdom and ways of God in both Old Testament and New Testament can blend in with the present leading of the living Christ and the Holy Spirit as the congregation engages in her pastoral care of demonized members or neighbors. The church cannot be writing a "now testament" of obedience and power unless she is listening constantly and deeply to the truest wisdom from the Scriptures.[6]

If the pastor has read with discernment in church history, he will be struck with the fact that classic church historians tend to play down exorcism. They do not make it central in the gospel, the kingdom of God, the movements of evangelism, the formation of liturgies, the writing of hymns, the assembling of creeds, the teaching of doctrine, the systematizations of theology, the expressions through art, the ministries through medicine, or the instruction programs for Christian nurture. Church historians like Philip Schaff, Kenneth Latourette, Hendrik Berkhof, Williston Walker, and Roland Bainton are examples of sober and balanced reporting.

He will notice a few other writers, many of them recent, who insist exorcism always was important and should be so now. In this way they justify their own focus upon the devil and their call to a "deliverance ministry." The wisdom and sanity of the centuries will help the pastor to be cautious, waiting for the word and leading of the living God to and through His people. Some persons will hail the eruption of the demonic as a sign of the near return of Jesus Christ to earth.[7]

It is interesting that similar convincement that the Christian is mistaken to give much attention to the devil have come from two vastly different approaches. Karl Barth, representing the climax of German biblical and theological scholarship of a certain era, devoted 152 pages in his *Church Dogmatics, Vol. III* (Edinburgh: T. & T. Clark, 1958) to angels, and then a mere ten to demons. He insisted that Satan is to be given only an avertive, sidewise glance by persons whose gaze is totally fixed on Almighty God.

H. W. Turner as he listened in on hundreds of African independent congregations found them busy emphasiz-

ing Christ's total victory at Calvary over all the demons
(Colossians 2:15) and building up a doctrine of good
angel visitations rather than demon possessions.[8]

Thus from believers newly delivered from animism
comes the implicit warning not to pay attention to the
father of lies. These young Christians are glad Christ has
delivered them from the fears of demons lurking and
indwelling here and there. They could teach some Christians from the Western world how to claim Christ's victory more totally and effectively.

*5. The pastor will take his stand with the apostles and
listen for God's present leading primarily through the
epistles.* Naturally he will agree that God's Son, Jesus
Christ, by "the finger of God," did cast out demons. He
did so strikingly different from the exorcisms of either
Greeks, Jews, Babylonians, Assyrians, or Egyptians.
The books of Matthew, Mark, and Luke show Christ's
unique ministry of exorcism.

But the humble pastor will hesitate to try to be a
present Messiah, with a "finger of God" to use. He will
observe that Christ did His exorcisms mostly outside of
Judea and seldom where God's people were most fully
taught. Within the Scriptures he will observe a trend
away from exorcism, with no mention at all of exorcisms
already in John's Gospel. When he comes to the pastoral
care assumptions of Christ's apostles as they served congregations through their epistles, he sees that God's
Spirit has led to a very different, non-exorcistic way of
helping demonized persons. Practical help is offered in
Christian love to very real problems and needs. But
formulas of exorcism are conspicuous by their absences.

In the epistles, the devil or Satan is mentioned alongside of suffering such as Paul's own thorn in the flesh (2 Corinthians 12:7), the widow's troubles (1 Timothy 5:15), the temptations of the novice pastor (1 Timothy 3:7), wrath nursed beyond sundown (Ephesians 4:26), the ability to control one's sex drives (1 Corinthians 7:5), and the tendency toward legalism (1 Timothy 4:1). When the temptation is to speak blasphemy, Paul uses excommunications of Hymenaeus and Alexander, but not exorcism (1 Timothy 1:20) even though modern exorcists now list blasphemy as a strong sign of the demon possession which calls for exorcism.[9]

6. *Pastoral leaders will observe that few of the demonized persons Christ ministered to were the violent type, supernaturally strong, speaking unknown languages, blasphemous, or clairvoyant.* They were not the uncontrollable kind of persons which modern exorcists and deliverance ministers have decreed are demon possessed. Congregational leaders see instead a weak woman bent low with infirmity (Luke 13:15), a fragile girl of Syrophoenicia (Mark 7:26), a dumb person unable to speak (Luke 11:14 or Matthew 9:32), a weak child falling into the fire (Mark 9:21), a stumbling blind man (Matthew 12:22), a person with loss of hearing (Mark 9:25), and a person who could neither see nor speak (Matthew 12:22). The case of antisocial behavior turns out to be almost the exception (Mark 5:1) and thus scarcely a model for pastoral care.

Christ rebukes the "demon" of these suffering people much as He rebuked the storm or the fever of a woman.[10]

Congregational leaders will hear, loud and clear, the warning of Christ against naming as a "demon" in someone else whatever it is that one hates. He protested when persons did this to John the Baptist (Matthew 11:18) or to the despised Samaritan (John 8:48) or when they said that He Himself was indwelt by Belzebub. This "naming the demon" brought Christ's warning of the unpardonable sin (Matthew 12:31). Solid biblical foundation seems lacking for the exorcists' terms of oppression, harassment, subjection, and possession.

The conflicting lists of demons cast out by modern exorcists, each so sure they alone are right and praising something the next one calls a demon, cautions the wise pastor against all naming of fleshly lusts or sicknesses as demons.[11]

7. As the pastor continues to use the example of the apostles as his model of pastoral care for "demonized" persons, he finds a non-exorcistic pattern through the epistles.[12]

Christ's warning to the disciples that "this kind cannot be driven out by anything but prayer" (Mark 9:29) was heard and applied by the apostles in their pastoral care of congregations. Paul prayed three times for deliverance from "a messenger of Satan," a thorn in the flesh, and then went on to claim victory in spite of it. He knew all about exorcism, but refused to rely upon it or use it in his own life.

Christ's teaching was familiar to James. He called for a sacred congregational ordinance, anointing a suffering member with oil, as the elders gather around hearing the confessions and praying the prayer of faith (James 5:13-

18). Prayer is absolutely central in this service which James doubtless intended as the replacement of exorcism rituals.

Likely Peter remembered that, when Satan desired to have him so that he might sift him as wheat, Christ's way to help was by prayer. So he urged casting anxieties upon God as a way of victory over "roaring lion" devils (1 Peter 5:8).

Paul urged that prayer and honesty surround the young pastor lest Satanic temptation come to him in the form of pride (1 Timothy 3:6). For his own deliverance from wicked and evil men, Paul asked for prayer (2 Thessalonians 3:1-3). Paul cites nine or ten persons who needed help and whose behavior caused him trouble, such as Demas; but never hints that an exorcism might help any of them.

The apostles recalled keenly that Christ had never used exorcism as a way to help any of them during their times of failure and sin. They remembered that He told them to encircle one another with mutual intercessory prayer, crying out together to God, "Deliver us from the evil one." And they founded congregations which relied upon one another's prayers. This was the deliverance ministry Christ intended.

The rare exception, when Paul adjured a demon to leave the slave girl at Philippi (Acts 16:18) seems seldom to be repeated, and was never assumed in dealing with troubled persons in the congregations of Corinth, Ephesus, Thessalonica, Rome, Phillipi, Lystra, and all of the rest.

The pastor is always more concerned that the Spirit's power be claimed for bringing repentance; for enabling faith; for filling rather than casting out; for enabling for life together as the body of Christ; for discerning the mind of the risen, reigning Christ; and for producing the fruit of the Spirit. If he follows the pattern implied in the epistles, he will not be naming demons, taking command, adjuring by Jesus and casting out discarnate spirits.

8. *A pastor instructed in the ways of the human is aware that too much talking about the devil only awakens men's worst fantasies and fears.* His own patient exegesis tells him that the favorite phrase of the exorcists, by which each claims that his discerning of the spirits is the right one, is a misinterpretation of 1 Corinthians 12:10. The pastor sees discerning of spirits (alongside of interpretation of tongues which follows it in Paul's list) as a gift to discern Spirit-given consensus, a gift given to discern and affirm a Spirit-given gift, and an ability to sense where God's Holy Spirit is at work in the congregational meeting. The context gives no warrant for concluding that it is specialized ability to name another person's demon.[13]

The pastor and congregation may call to repentance a person who belittles the redemptive value of Christ's sufferings on the cross (Matthew 16:23), or who is considering some betrayal of Christ for a paltry thirty pieces of silver (Matthew 27:3).

The pastor may tell some modern Pharisee, "You are of your father, the devil" (John 8:44) but will call the person to repent. If a modern Ananias is lying to God's Spirit in the area of stewardship (Acts 5:3) the pastor will call the person to repent and not resort to exorcism.

The power of God's Spirit in the gathered congregation may smite the liar with deep conviction.

Even when the pastor meets some modern "child of the devil" who functions like Elymas of old, he will not use exorcism but will call him to repent (Acts 13:10).

9. Wise pastoral leaders warn against dabbling in the occult. They will keep out of the debate on which activities or objects represent the occult and should be avoided by Christians who have no use for magic in any of its forms. Some insist that hypnotism, water dousing, or psychoanalysis are demonic and occult and to be avoided. Others omit these and create their own list of taboos. Some go so far as to avoid carvings and artifacts from certain countries they regard as "heathen" and thus likely to be an idol. Each expert is very sure he is right, and almost all differ from one another. One expert lists 157 demons he has named, and another has passed the 200 mark.

The wise pastor takes his stand with Paul in 1 Corinthians 8:4, "We know that 'an idol has no real existence,' " and in 1 Corinthians 10:20, "I do not want you to be partners with demons." Objects and rituals known to be actively aligned with and utilized by devil worshipers should have no appeal to people in whose life Jesus is Lord. A lot of the "doubtful stuff" which tends toward the magical should be avoided as well. But the pastor who fears objects and artifacts seems to be betraying a kind of superstitution the prophets and apostles did not share.

The pastor refuses to lapse into a neo-animism which sees a demon lurking everywhere. In areas which might be neutral, his attitude may be more like Paul's in 1 Timothy 4:4, 5, "For everything created by God is good, and nothing is to be rejected if it is received with thanksgiving; for then it is consecrated by the word of God and prayer." Since God "has the whole wide world in His hand," Christians are not afraid of powers, height, depth, things present, things to come, nor anything in all creation.

In view of the harm which well-meaning but misinformed exorcists seem to be doing to people they serve, the pastor may need to warn against some of their operations as much as he warns against Ouija boards.[14]

10. Wise pastoral leaders maintain continual dialogue with competent psychiatrists of the area. Any competent psychiatrist can diagnose many weird phenomena in personality. If psychiatrists are not committed Christians, they usually are satisfied with a psychiatric diagnosis, and work toward healing with appropriate use of drugs and therapy. If in addition to being thoroughly trained psychiatrists they are also committed Christians, they probably will combine fervent prayers with their therapeutic care, even though they know the psychiatric diagnostic terms for all the phenomena, which exorcists insist are purely demonic. Psychiatrists are well aware that both physical and emotional disorders can trigger man's ultimate anxieties and cause him to take a fresh position toward his Maker and his destiny.

One of the most hopeful situations in pastoral care of demonized persons is the humble cooperation of pastors—who know the heritage of the Christian faith in its biblical and historical depth, whose own lives bear the

authenticating marks of the fruit of the Spirit, whose
faith and reliance upon God's power and Spirit are
childlike, and whose dependence upon the intercessory
power of God's praying people is strong—with psychiatrists who bring their dedicated personalities, their grasp
of the science of medicine, their understanding of what
forms and deforms mind and emotions, their clinically-
based understanding of the therapeutic use of drugs, and
their specialized styles of counseling.[15]

It was toward such a happy cooperation which the
Apostle James pointed when he urged using oil, which
symbolized their best medicine. Led by the elders, who
represented the praying congregation, the sick should be
anointed with oil amidst the prayers of confession and
of faith.

In such an approach, the sick and suffering (physical,
mental, or spiritual) will always be given the best of
God's gifts through nature and science (oil) together
with what God gives through super-nature (prayer).
Medicine may partake more of the laws of nature and
prayer more of the power of the resurrection, but both
are ours in Christ. "All things are yours, and you are
Christ's, and Christ is God's." The highest ideal would
be to have Christian doctors and psychiatrists, who are
members of the congregation, to join in the anointing
with oil, service of prayer, and confession.

*11. The wise pastor will seek for more wholesome ways
to identify deviant behavior than to quickly call it
"demons."* He will find more prophetic ways to oppose
sin and the disruptive forces in the group. As rapid
change frightens the group and new forces which are evil

threaten, he will try to avoid focusing on one disturbed member, naming his embodiment of the group's problem a demon, and casting it out of him by an exorcism ritual. This is the way non-Christian religions utilize exorcism, but the movement Jesus launched has other and better ways to conquer the evil one.

Rather, the pastor will encourage the entire congregation to speak to one another honestly about encroaching sin. He will warn against going to bed mad and thus giving place to the devil (Ephesians 4:26). He will encourage the entire brotherhood to walk out into the light, as he is in the light, so that the blood of Jesus Christ can go on cleansing from sin. He will rely upon brotherly admonition, pastoral counseling, the word and sacrament in worship, and the celebration of Christ's victory throughout the Christian year to aid in Christian victory.

There must be more wholesome ways, more tender ways, more biblical ways, more nurturing ways for the group to update its ethics, to sensitize the conscience against wrong, to rally the support of the group, and to stand together against the devil than the exorcism rituals now being used by so many "deliverance ministers." The congregational life pictured in Ephesians 6:11-20 shows an emphasis upon the teaching of the truth; a concern for discerning God's right way (righteousness); an active ministry of spreading peace; a total response to Christ as Savior and Lord (faith); experiencing God's saving action from time to time in the group (salvation); and hearing God's Word (Scripture) preached and taught so that it divides asunder the thoughts and intents of hearts. All the while the group carries one another in intense mutual intercessory prayer. This picture of congregational life and meetings is presented as the way to "stand against the wiles of the devil."[16]

12. Rather than becoming fearful of discarnate spirits and identifying demons in everybody, the pastor will follow the apostle's example and speak most about the "big demons." Just as Isaiah (in chapter 14) and Ezekiel (in chapter 28) saw kingship itself as the most demonic "principality and power" around them, so Paul told the Ephesian congregation to watch the "big demons" (Ephesians 6:11-20). They were to wrestle more against the influence of the demonized power structures than against mere "flesh and blood" demons, such as a church member might risk giving place to if he allowed the sun to go down upon his wrath (Ephesians 4:26).[17]

One can imagine that the Ephesus congregation understood the "principalities and powers" as the structure formed when persons enslaved by evil banded together into institutions. In Ephesus all of the countervailing powers of society (big government represented by the city clerk, big business represented by Demetrius, big labor represented by the crowd which yelled Diana's praises for two hours, and big religion represented by the Diana priests and exorcists) were aligned to foster the Diana myth. The Ephesian brothers and sisters were in danger of taking in portions of this value system, almost with the air they breathed. Truly the mass media of their day, and the economic system in which they lived their lives, were demonized.

One of the first items on the congregational agenda of Ephesus was to stand together about the wily, subtle inroads of these false value systems. They discussed the ways in which Christ would lead them to a discipleship lifestyle different from the lifestyle in their city.

Other examples of structured evil might be the caste system, Hitler's racism, white racism in the Bible Belt or South Africa, godless communism or capitalism, or the military-industrial complex. Congregations need to discuss often and stand together against the wily seduction of demonic ideas which comes in through structured evils of their times, through advertising, through patriotism, through exploitations, through people-crushing systems, through principalities and powers. A principality and power seems to be some instrument God created, an institution He allowed, but which is now functioning as God's adversary.

Even in coping with structured evil, God's people cannot always be doing an "Elijah on Mt. Carmel" stand. Herman Riffel tells of a black woman Baptist pastor of Philadelphia who "sent her people out around the riot area and took authority over the evil forces that caused the people to hate each other, in that way quieting the area around her church." This certainly was confronting the powers![18]

William Stringfellow suggests that the most vigorous act of Christian exorcism which has been done in America for a long time was the pouring of napalm on a collection of draft records.[19]

Hendrik Berkhof, in his masterful treatment of principalities and powers suggests that the church can exert such prophetic presence and pressure in society that a demonic mammon shrinks down to finances, and a Nazism can be reduced to a mere "ism," an idea still in the air but unable to destroy helpless people.[20]

Some sidewalk theologians and concerned Christians have been asking if the Watergate trials and the expulsion of dishonesty in the White House might be a recent exorcism of the principalities and powers. Roman Catholic and Protestant pastors in Denver, Colorado, area appealed that national flags be removed from sanctuaries to exorcize all symbols of competing loyalties.[21]

In the biblical view of history, God will fit even the rebellious principalities and powers into His ultimate victory and cause them to bring glory to the reigning Christ, even in spite of themselves. It is part of a pastor's goal that, even now, God's power through Christ in His church may astound the principalities and powers (Ephesians 3:10).

Although the pastoral team cannot fully grasp all that the apostles meant by principalities and powers, they sense that they did not seem to be implying etherial, discarnate spirits, flitting invisibly through the air, waiting to enter and to take possession of innocent children, anxious nuns, the weak, physically suffering persons, or Spirit-filled Christians as soon as they in any way grieve the Spirit.

Rather, the pastoral team looks for systematized and institutionalized evil which many persons who refuse to accept Christ's lordship help to form. The Apostle Paul felt that principalities and powers are part of God's creation (Colossians 1:16) although in some way rebelling against God. They don't fully sense what God is doing (1 Corinthians 2:6-13). But these powers can fascinate and captivate persons who give their loyalty to them (Ephesians 2:12). In some vicinities congregational leaders may see in the Mafia such organized evil. In some slum areas the evil powers may appear to be the dope pushers or the exploiting landlords.

The Christ of Calvary has publicly displayed His power over them (Colossians 2:15), although Christians must still resist their wiles and wrestle against their values and assumptions (Ephesians 6:12). Only at the end of history will the powers really cast their crowns at the feet of God's Son (Revelation 5:10, 11).

In Christ's body and life, believers cannot be coerced or controlled by the powers. They can never separate Christians from Christ's love now (Romans 8:38). Christ will eventually destroy all of these alien centers of power and influence (1 Corinthians 15:51-58).

In almost any area congregational leaders will need to stand together against the wiles of a nationalism or patriotism which usurps Christ's lordship in members' lives. The idol-demon of materialism is all pervasive, oppressive, and the root of all evil in all parts of the affluent West. Culture religion, which assumes that the cultural status quo is the will of God, can easily become an all-pervasive power for evil.

13. The pastor will avoid the sensational. When Paul met with the pastoral elders of the Ephesus congregation (see Acts 20) to review his ministry among them, he completely ignored the exorcisms performed by handkerchiefs taken from his person. He stressed the solid and abiding ministries of repentance and faith which he had kept central in his work.[22]

This may well be the pattern for the pastor. God's Spirit will always be sovereign and may choose to send something startling and even sensational as he did with Paul's hanky-exorcisms. But the wise pastor will not keep referring to it. He will not try to build a reputation as a "deliverance minister" upon it. He will know that, unless solid steps of repentance for known sin are followed by realistic steps of faith and commitment, any exorcism of the person's demon is most likely to leave the person helpless against the next attack, a house empty into which seven worse demons soon return. One evangelical psychiatrist, who prays with his patients as well as employs professional therapy, reports that the euphoria of the demonized who are delivered by some modern exorcists actually lasted about three weeks.

A congregation allowed to keep saying, "The devil made me do it," and to keep relying upon a messianic-type exorcist to come along and "take command" in a deliverance ministry, is most likely to become more weak, more unstable, and more confused. A congregation whose members learn to take responsibility for their own lusts, who learn to admonish one another in love so repentance can be kept up to date, who learn to walk in the power and fullness of the Holy Spirit, and who insist upon utilizing God's gifts of medicine and psychiatry, will almost certainly be more wholesome, more whole, and more genuinely victorious in their Christian lives than those served by exorcism.

Many observers have remarked how the symptoms shown by possessed people almost always mirror what they have been taught by the exorcists. One disturbing disclosure is how closely the rituals Christian exorcists have developed compare with the rituals currently used by the exorcists in non-Christian religions.

14. The pastoral focus will be on Christ and only very rarely and obliquely upon the devil. By noting only a few of the many instances from the apostles, this pattern for victory is readily apparent.

The apostles tell of victory after victory of believers through the power of Christ and the working of His Spirit. Sometimes Paul expects that the victory will come simply, without sharp struggle. He gives the breathtaking promise that if we are "wise as to what is good and guileless as to what is evil; then the God of peace will soon crush Satan under your feet" (Romans 16:19, 20). Paul also says, "Be betrothed to Christ, and Satan cannot beguile you as he did Eve through his subtlety" (2 Corinthians 11:1-4, paraphrased). He tells us that Christ disarmed evil powers (Colossians 2:15).

John the revelator promises that believers can overcome the accuser of the brethren by being radically committed to Christ (loving not their lives even unto death), by giving their testimony fearlessly, and by relying upon the love of Christ evidenced by the giving of His life's blood (Revelation 12:7-12).

Jude cautions that just denouncing, reviling, and ridiculing the devil (as many deliverance ministers seem led to do) is not a good way to help one another to victory. He speaks of convincing the doubter, rescuing the endangered, building one another up in faith, and praying in the Holy Ghost (Jude 9, 19-23).

James reminds of the image of God, the Spirit God has given to us and over which He yearns; of the increasing grace God waits to give, so that by his own Spirit-enabled will the believer can resist the devil and make him flee. He stresses that the first secret of victory is to refuse any copout, but to take responsibility for one's own lusts (James 1:13-15; 4:5-10).

The writer of Hebrews never hints that the congregation should rely on an exorcist to discern and name demons. Instead, he urges that, as part of spiritual growth, every member be trained by the practice of decision-making to discern good and evil (Hebrews 5:14).

Peter urges victory over even the "roaring lion" kind of devilish attack, by attitudes of humility and trust, a firm resisting, relying upon the God of all grace to restore, establish, and strengthen through the whole experience of testing, reproach, or suffering (1 Peter 5:6-11).

Timothy is urged, as a pastor, to keep his watchful eyes upon actual evil men who are deceiving and being deceived (2 Timothy 3:13). That may be the truest way to "name the demons"! Paul assures Pastor Timothy that the exorcist types, like Jannes and Jambres, who finally could not keep standing up to Moses and his ministry of absolute monotheism power, will not get very far now either (2 Timothy 3:7-9). But he never suggests exorcising a demon from an individual. Rather Paul tells Pastor Timothy to help persons escape from the snare of the devil after being captured by him to do his will by remaining a teacher and not by becoming an exorcist, by continuing to be forebearing, by confronting the troubled person himself as an "opponent," relying all the while upon God to grant the troubled person repentance, as a person "gets awake again" and comes to know the truth (2 Timothy 2:24-26).[23]

To the pastor of the Ephesus congregation, so rife with exorcism in its background and present environment, Paul outlines a procedure to help persons escape from the snare of the devil, which is solidly pastoral at every point. It is also the opposite from the usual exorcistic ritual at almost every point. The assumptions and method Paul outlines for Timothy, the young pastor, fit beautifully with the anointing with oil-prayer-confession ordinance which James in 5:13-18 urged for the congregation. Paul apparently would be comfortable with the developed science of medicine and psychiatry which God's loving Spirit has also given for man's total health and wholeness. In Paul's instruction to Timothy, there is no naming or addressing the demon, no taking command.

There may continue to be situations, as with Paul's exorcising of the demonized slave girl at Philippi, when the church will need to resort temporarily to exorcistic ritual, taking command of the demon and commanding him to depart. This can be a way the method of healing is temporarily adapted to the expectations of the suffering person (Acts 16:18). But the pastor will quickly return to the constant themes of pastoral care which recur in the epistles. There is absolutely no hint in the epistle to the Philippians, where hopefully the converted slave girl became a member, that exorcisms were to be used to help Euodia and Syntyche or any demonized members in trouble (Philippians 4:2).

15. Pastoral patience will be needed when exorcists are working secretly in the congregation. In most eruptions of exorcism the experts are not settled pastors, but like the seven sons of Sceva, itinerants who serve outside their own congregation. Many are deeply devout and sincerely desire to exalt Jesus Christ and His saving power. Some have discovered their exorcistic gift accidentally.

Even though there is some evidence that unsettled, unstable, nervous, and power-hungry persons seem to be rather numerous among the exorcists, the wise pastor does not call undue attention to this fact. After all, many people thought God's prophets in Bible times were a bit strange. Many persons whom God mightily used during church history, such as George Fox, Martin Luther, or John Wesley, had eccentric characteristics. God does use "the weak things of the world" and may do so again if He wills. God's prophets would scarcely fit a beautiful balanced B. F. Skinner behaviorally produced model![24]

Although God led His people away from ritual exorcisms (deliverance from demons by adjurations and appeals to a higher power) both by the prophets in the Old Testament and the apostles in the New Testament, should not insist that God will never do His own work of grace, His own forgiving, His own delivering, and His own strengthening through the modern deliverance minister or Christian exorcist. The Apostle Paul believed that God might bless some hearer of the gospel, even though the preacher wanted to "add affliction to Paul's bonds" as one of the reasons why he preached! If the present-day pastor has that same awed sense of God's determination to help and to bless, then he can believe that blessings can come through exorcisms even though they seem less than God's first and highest will for the pastoral care of His people. The pastoral team will not allow themselves to be diverted into opposing itinerant exorcists or stressing their inconsistencies.

The wise and patient pastor does not allow the congregation or community to conclude that it is really the exorcists and deliverance ministers who "believe in miracles" and whose faith produces "instant" ones here and now. If his own faith is biblically informed and Holy Spirit renewed he will not only accept with childlike faith the miracles of creation, incarnation, regeneration, and resurrection. He will live by the thousands of quiet miracles God's Spirit works through love-changed relationships, wise medical care, worship, and godly living and nurture.

Great pastoral patience and skill will be needed to rightly interpret God's quiet miracles alongside His more startling ones. The team of medical specialists the Roman Catholic Church has appointed to apply rigorous tests to the claims of miracles at the healing shrine at Lourdes, France, have found that "perhaps no more than one percent achieve what they consider permanent cures."[25]

The wise and biblically informed congregational leaders may well ask the Christian exorcist or deliverance minister just why his world seems to have so many more demons in it than angels! If God is really omnipotent and His living Spirit and angels are everywhere present and active, why doesn't the exorcist stress the hopeful possibilities of being assisted by a guardian angel? In the biblical record God's people were much more aware of angels and in communication with them than they were involved in exorcising demons. Why doesn't the Christian exorcist also become aware of angels, speak of them, rely upon their help, and talk more about them than he does about demons?[26]

In fairness, it should be reasserted that many deliverance ministers help strengthen some good and needed emphases in the church. They often bring a fervor, an earnestness, a spontaneity in testimony, a concern for sufferers, a firm belief in God's power, a reliance in the power of prayer, and a love for the study of the Scriptures. They do, however, tend to lead people to expect instant deliverance from any and every ill.

Rather than the instant deliverance, the startling miracle, and the casting out of the demon by exorcism, the pastor and congregational leaders offer the patient, quiet, continuous, nurturing work of scriptural teaching, step-by-step repentance, growth in grace, and daily reliance upon both the fruit and gifts of the Holy Spirit in the congregation. Strong biblical preaching and teaching can strengthen against satanic attack. Most church members will not assimilate a ponderous warning that they "should encounter their finitude but not relate to it as final!" They need strong and constant teaching against materialism that can prepare for victory over the satanic suggestion that "these stones be made bread."

A well-rounded instruction about the place and right uses of power will strengthen against the desire to get all the glory and power of earth's kingdoms. A constant nurture program which interprets God's loving providential care in the midst of His laws of cause-and-effect will prepare congregational members to rise above the seductive desire to be the exception, to live a cushioned existence, to imagine that although other people would dash their feet against a stone if they leaped from a pinnacle yet God owes it to them to somehow make them the exception from His laws for human beings. Much exorcism and occultism around the world arises from man's attempts to manipulate the supernatural, to be the exception, to deny his humanness, and to refuse limits.

Clear teaching will be needed lest some modern Job begins to doubt God's love when adversity comes, or when a tempter (even in the form of a well-meaning healer) hints that if you were really a saint your body could never be sick![27]

Profound issues of life's ultimate meaning and destiny will need to be taught constantly in the congregation to offset demonism. People are still deeply disturbed when they honestly allow themselves Eve's hope, "You shall not surely die." People are deeply tempted when they honestly conclude that self-discipline is a hard way of life, since everything they enjoy most is either illegal, fattening, or sinful! Teaching people to take ownership of their bodily drives, appetites, and lusts, and to find the freedoms and fulfillment a covenanting community of disciples can offer, can be the surest way to resist the devil. After all, Paul summarizes one of the greatest statements ever given to the church, the Book of Romans, with the words, "I would have you wise as to what is good and guileless as to what is evil; then the God of peace will soon crush Satan under your feet (Romans 16:19, 20).

If congregational leaders feel led by God's Spirit to call the congregation to united prayer for a deeply troubled or demonized member, the anointing-with-oil service outlined by the Apostle James has biblical foundation, embodies sound pastoral principles, and serves to renew the depth of the entire congregational life of caring for one another.[28]

Congregations which stand closer to the sacramental tradition may wish to link their prayers for one another more closely to the sacramental center of their life and fellowship. The International Order of Saint Luke, the Physician has developed a *Clergy Manual for Christian Healing.* The 1973 edition contains a "Form for Divine Exorcism." This manual is the result of the careful conferring of many mature leaders and attempts to link services closely to the life of the congregation and its prayer groups. It does not at all build its ritual upon the exceptional case reported in Mark 5:1-20 as so many deliverance ministers unfortunately do.

The manual includes a "Prayer for Claiming Deliverance" (p. 37), suggested by Derek Prince, in which the demonized person says, "In the name of Jesus I expel all evil spirits—I command them to leave me—I loose myself from them according to the Word of God and in the name of Jesus. Amen."

The manual may move too near to the exorcistic pattern of naming demons in one another and adjuring the demons to depart, so that congregational leaders will feel it falls short of the pastoral care for demonized people which Christ's apostles implied in the epistles of the New Testament. If, however, congregational leaders come to a very rare case when they feel that the drastic confrontational approaches of the exorcism ritual are wise and justified, the manual's suggestions are certainly preferable to those of many solitary exorcists who travel about.[29]

3
Are You Celebrating
Our Lord's Ascension?

When Paul reminded the Ephesus congregation of Christ's triumphant ascension he quoted from Psalm 68:18. He reminded them that the Holy Spirit gifts the ascending Lord gave (and keeps giving) to the congregation, are actually part of the powers He took away from the defeated foe. Paul wanted the congregation to celebrate Christ's ascension in the spirit of the great coronation psalms of Israel's worship.

Whenever a triumphant conqueror came home, the still unconquered kings hastened to bring their tribute to him. Thus he had not only the plunder taken from the kings he had just conquered, but also the tribute gifts voluntarily brought by the remaining kings of the areas. If his conquest was massive and the gifts of tribute also great, the conquering king became unbelievably wealthy and powerful. There was literally a redistribution of the world's resources and power (Psalm 68:31).

Good kings did not keep this all for themselves, but turned at once and "gave gifts" to their loyal soldiers who had shared in the victory and had risked their lives to achieve it. Suddenly they became unbelievably rich, too. They were elevated above the power and wealth of the tribute-paying rulers of the area.

In Colossians 2:15 Paul exulted that Christ's victory stripped demonic forces of their powers. In Ephesians 4:8 he asserted that these powers are now given to the congregation as charismatic gifts and enablements for ministry. Believers who have faith to accept their share of Christ's victorious ascension are now astoundingly rich. Their relationships to the forces of the enemy (defeated by the ascended Christ) are completely reset. They will not deal with one of Satan's imps any more than Moses would have argued with one of Pharaoh's officers after the Exodus!

Because the apostles, led by God's Spirit, grasped by faith the fact that cosmic powers were shifted when Christ ascended, they never, in any of their epistles to young churches, urged believers to do battle with demons by exorcism. Although Christ had expelled them by His bare word of power, after His ascension He empowered His followers to claim victory in another way.

As believers discern and claim the Spirit gifts the ascended Christ keeps giving, they conquer the already-vanquished and depleted principalities and powers by gathering for worship. There they regird themselves with God's whole armor. Using the gifts of wisdom, knowledge, hospitality, and all the other helps the reigning Lord waits to give, they withstand in any evil day. They claim God's salvation (present saving action), explore the Word of God as given in the sacred Scriptures, reequip themselves with the gospel of peace, and encircle one another with intercessory prayer. As they do this in congregational worship, they are claiming His promised power from on high. They are being strengthened with the might of their sovereign, ascended Lord. His gifts conquer the world rulers of this present darkness (Ephesians 6:10-20). He gives victory as in congregational prayer for one another believers ask Him to "deliver us from the evil one." This is the way the reigning Lord has given His people to supersede His earthly exorcism way.

Every worship service should have in it some celebration of Christ's ascension. When John worshiped in the Spirit on the Lord's day, he saw his ascended Lord much as He had appeared when the disciples saw Him last. Then His shining face had blended in with the sun shining in its strength. John knew again that his reigning Lord held the keys of hell and of death. He was careful to share his own glimpse of Christ's glory with other worshipers (Revelation 1:9-18).

If another worshiper is being driven to his limits by persecution, he may (like Stephen) be granted a glimpse of heaven opened, and of his Lord standing at God's right hand (Acts 7:56). During "concerns of the church time" members should keep sharing the ways their reigning Lord is coming through to them in all their need.

Paul was concerned that Christ's ascension and present sovereignty be celebrated in song. He liked the early church hymn, cited in Philippians 2:7-11, in which the church sang of every knee bowing before the exalted Christ. They included every name or power, in every realm, and by faith took their own position in Christ's victorious reign. Early church hymns, as reflected in the

Book of Revelation, also reveals this same celebration of Christ's ascension.

Celebrating Christ's ascension should help worshipers to return to our daily work where we do not yet see "everything put under him." Here Christians serve amidst unbelievers being taken captive by Satan at his will. Believers need to regather, even the two or three who meet in Christ's name, to seek Christ's will about a matter. Here their risen Lord will hold rendezvous. Here they can catch a glimpse of their reigning Lord and be changed into His image from one level of glory and victory to a still higher one. Here they can testify to one another in the words of Hebrews 2:9, "We see Jesus . . . crowned with glory and honor."

We celebrate our Lord's ascension and present reign in our fellowship when we help one another to find victory over satanic attacks. The gifts our reigning Lord is giving are precisely what our brother and sister are needing. A suffering widow may indeed be straying after Satan, but Christ's gifts of helps, hospitality, administration, and the like, are precisely His way to help the widow to victory (1 Timothy 5:15). If a pastor is being puffed up with pride, as Paul cited in 1 Timothy 3:6, 7, it may be seen as a snare of the devil. But the ascended Christ will give the brotherhood the gifts the faltering pastor needs. The church needs nothing more than the enabling gifts from Christ and the fruit of His Holy Spirit to be assured of victory.

The ascended Christ is still gifting His church with the powers He took from the foe He defeated by His death, His resurrection, and His ascension. If anyone is taken captive by Satan at his will, we should use Christ's gift of

Spirit-empowered teaching as Paul told Timothy to do (2 Timothy 2:24-26). If a believer feels he or she has a "thorn in the flesh" which is becoming a "messenger of Satan," the gifted congregation should help the believer to find victory by prayer as Paul did (2 Corinthians 12:7-9). If a believer resists, the devil must flee (James 4:7). He knows the power the ascended Christ is giving to the humblest believer.

If a faltering believer shrinks back to pre-ascension ways, and wants to assign one of his own "lusts of the flesh" to Satan, we do not endorse this. With the Apostle James we insist that, because of the ascension, Christ's follower can personally say as Jesus did, "Get thee behind me, Satan." We do not honor the ascended Christ as fully as we ought if we refuse to believe the extent to which He has depleted the enemy. Just as Moses did not condescend to name Pharaoh's highest officers after the victory of the Exodus, so we do not honor Satan's imps by being interested in their names.

In conclusion, we celebrate Christ's ascension when we claim His intercession for us when we pray. We celebrate Christ's ascension when we sing of His present exaltation above every principality and power. We celebrate Christ's ascension when we take the gifts He took from our vanquished foe and use them to continue in Christ's victory.

We celebrate Christ's victory when we remain guile-less as to evil powers, relying upon our Lord to crush Satan under our feet (Romans 12:20). We claim His victory by praising Him for it in advance. As far as we are concerned, Christ is heir of all things. Principalities and powers are subject to Him. He is upholding all things by the Word of His power. He is seated at the right hand of the majesty on high. Nothing can separate us from His love. Satan's works are destroyed (1 John 3:8). We who believe are moved over into His kingly reign (Acts 26:18).

We keep celebrating the reality that all spirits are subject to Him. He is likely to send angelic, ministering spirits to assist us who are heirs of salvation (Hebrews 2:14).

Are you celebrating Christ's reception of gifts when He ascended? Are you exulting that He received the powers stripped from the kingdom of evil? Are you praising Him because His enemies are being made His footstool? Are you believing that all authority is already given to Him in heaven and earth?

Thank God, we do not need to live in fear of the evil one. Christ has overcome the serpent.

Notes

Preface

1. John Nicola, technical consultant for the film, *The Exorcist,* explains the official Roman Catholic ritual of exorcism in *Diabolical Possession and Exorcism* (Rockford, Ill.: Tan Books, 1974), pp. 169-172.

2. *The Clergy Manual for Christian Healing* (Logansport, Ind.: St. Luke's Press, 1973).

3. Reinhold Seeburg, *History of Doctrines,* p. 246.

Part I

Chapter 1: God Controls My Life

1. For the rest of the list of 158 demons which Don Basham has exorcized as he reports it, see his book *A Manual of Spiritual Warfare* (Greensburg, Pa.; Manna Books, 1974), pp. 42, 43.

2. See T. H. Gaster, in *The Interpreter's Dictionary of the Bible,* Vol. IV, pp. 224-228.

3. See T. H. Gaster, "Angels," in *The Interpreter's Dictionary of the Bible,* Vol. 1, pp. 129-134.

Chapter 2: God Limits What the Devil Can Do to Me

1. See James Kallas, *The Real Satan* (Minneapolis: Augsburg, 1975), pp. 50 ff.

2. Hendrik Berkhof in *Christ and the Powers* (Scottdale, Pa.: Herald Press, 1962) has given the clearest statement of the limiting of the demonic powers.

Chapter 3: God Tests Me to Strengthen Me

1. For a discussion of the radical subordination taught in the *"Haustafeln"* passages, see John H. Yoder, *The Politics of Jesus* (Grand Rapids: Eerdmans, 1972).

Chapter 6: I Don't Have to Fear Demons

1. Jean La Fontaine in her report on "Witchcraft and Sorcery in Bugisu" in Middleton and Winter's book *Witchcraft and Sorcery in East Africa* (New York: Frederick and Praeger, 1964) says, "Formerly . . . all deaths were believed to be the result of witchcraft and sorcery," p. 191.

2. Middleton and Winter, *op. cit.*, p. 20.

3. T. H. Gaster does many word studies on the prophet's use of the words their neighbors used for demons. See *The Interpreter's Dictionary of the Bible,* Vol.I pp. 817-824.

Chapter 8: God's Son Defeated the Devil Decisively

1. For a careful study and comparison of the healing-exorcism narratives in the synoptic gospels see Lawrence J. McGinley, *Form Criticism of the Synoptic Healing Narratives* (Maryland: Woodstock College Press, 1944).

2. Here see S. Estrem's *Some Notes on the Demonology in the New Testament.*

Chapter 13. The Big Demons Oppress Me Most

1. Don Basham, *A Manual for Spiritual Welfare* (Greensburg, Pa.: Manna Books, 1974), pp. 42, 43.

2. Glenna Henderson, *My Name Is Legion* (Minneapolis: Bethany Fellowship, 1972).

Chapter 15: I Don't Accept the Alibi, "The Devil Made Me Do It"

1. Kurt Koch's formulas in *Christian Counseling and Occultism* (Grand Rapids: Kregel, 1965) are examples on the Christian side; Clark Offner and Henry Van Straeden, in *Modern Japanese Religions* (New York: Twayne, 1963) provide illustrations from non-Christian religions.

2. For a more extensive discussion of Christ's counseling methods see Robert Leslie, *Jesus and Logotherapy* (New York: Abingdon Press, 1965).

Part II

Chapter 1: Questions and Answers

1. Dr. R. Kenneth McAll, "The Ministry of Deliverance," *Expository Times,* July 1975, p. 297.

2. T. K. Oesterreich, *Possession: Demoniacal and Other* (New York: University Books, 1966), p. 379.

Chapter 2: Pastoral Care of Demonized Persons

1. See Daniel Day Williams, *The Minister and the Care of Souls* (New York: Harper and Bros. 1961), for a statement of pastoral care.

2. See Richard Woods, *The Occult Revolution* (New York: Seabury Press, 1973), for a portrayal of the contemporary situation.

3. See T. W. Davies, *Magic, Divination, and Demonology Among the Heb-*

rews and Their Neighbors (New York: Ktav Publishing Co., 1969).

4. Stanley and Ruth Freed, *Magic, Witchcraft, and Curing* (New York: Natural History Press, 1967), is one of many such reports.

5. T. K. Oesterreich's 400-page book, *Possession: Demoniacal and Other* (New York: University Books, 1966), is a thorough treatment.

6. John H. Yoder, *The Politics of Jesus* (Grand Rapids: Eerdmans, 1973), shows Christ's intention to create a new people now.

7. Merrill F. Unger, *Demons in the World Today* (Wheaton: Tyndale House, 1971), is one such writer.

8. H. W. Turner, *Profile Through Preaching* (London: Edinburgh House, 1965), a study of sermon texts used in a West African independent church.

9. Kurt E. Koch has written seven full-length books dealing with one aspect or another of *Occult Bondage and Deliverance.* Representative of them all is one by the above title, released in 1970 by Evangelical Publishers, West Germany. He draws his pattern largely from the exorcism narrative of Mark 5:1-20.

10. See Lawrence J. McGinley, *Form Criticism of the Synoptic Healing Narratives* (Maryland: Woodstock College Press, 1944). Furthermore, one of the few times disincarnate demons (the "frog kind," in this case) are said to go abroad and to enter into people is during the tribulation (Revelation 16:13).

11. Don Basham, *Manual for Spiritual Warfare* (Greensburg, Pa.: Manna Books, 1974), is one example of many other recent exorcists who insist upon the naming of demons.

12. See Eduard Schweizer, *Church Order in the New Testament* (London: SCM Press, 1961).

13. See Henry A. Kelly, *The Devil, Demonology, and Witchcraft* (New York: Doubleday, 1974). Professor Kelly devoted forty years to his study of the subject of demonology.

14. For those interested in psychical research, among the better treatments is the one by Martin Ebon, *The Devil's Bride* (New York: Harper & Row, 1974). Ebon has served as editor of a magazine devoted to psychical research entitled *Spiritual Frontiers.* The pastoral team does not really expect psychical research to solve the occultism problem.

15. Peter S. Ford, MD, has written a book urging pastoral-psychiatric cooperation, *The Healing Trinity* (New York: Harper & Row, 1971).

16. C. Norman Kraus, *The Healing Christ* (Scottdale, Pa.: Herald Press, 1972), points toward the wholeness. This was urged as the right way for the Ephesus congregation. They had witnessed the abortive exorcism methods of the seven sons of Sceva who adjured by Jesus. There is never a hint, in either Ephesians or First or Second Timothy, that they ever used adjuration exorcism again.

17. Hendrik Berkhof, *Christ and the Powers* (Scottdale, Pa.: Herald Press, 1962), is a helpful treatment of principalities and powers.

18. Herman H. Riffel, *A Living, Loving Way: Christian Maturity and the Spirit's Power* (Minneapolis: Bethany Fellowship, 1973).

19. William Stringfellow, *An Ethic for Christians and Other Aliens in a*

Strange Land (Waco: Word Books, 1973).

20. Berkhof, *op. cit.,* p. 40.

21. John W. Montgomery in his *Principalities and Powers* (Minneapolis: Bethany Fellowship, 1973), has documented bits of "hidden history" from many cultures, tracing the varied theories of organized evil which lay behind events, and rituals used to manipulate the supernatural.

22. The Swiss psychiatrist and pastor, Bernard Martin, demonstrates a therapeutic pastoral stance in his book, *Healing for You* (Richmond, Va.: John Knox, 1965).

23. Glenna Henderson in *My Name Is Legion* (Minneapolis: Bethany Fellowship, 1972), tells her experience of being exorcized by "demon-naming methods."

24. Robert W. Pelton and Karen Carden, *Snake Handlers: God Fearers? or Fanatics?* (New York: Nelson, 1974).

25. See *Faith Healing: Finger of God? or Scientific Curiosity?* by the team of medical doctors Claude A. Frazier, L. Nelson Bell, and Morris Fisbein, (New York: Nelson, 1973). Yet the one percent of authentic, uncontestable miracles remain, amidst 99 percent of credulity, suggestibility, and even superstition. And one percent of real help is enough to keep the quest going! The same is likely true of exorcism as a means of pastoral care of deeply disturbed, demonized members of the congregation. They may be ministering real and lasting help to one percent too. The concerned pastor is glad to see demonized people helped.

26. Morton Kelsey's monograph, *Dreams, the Dark Speech of the Spirit* (New York: Doubleday, 1974), might well be required reading for congregational leaders whose members have been exposed to either occultism or exorcism. Kelsey calls God's people to come to terms again with angel visitation and influencing.

27. Helmut Thielicke, *Between God and Satan* (Grand Rapids: Eerdmans, 1958).

28. Suggestions for conducting this service are given in my booklet, *How God Heals* (Scottdale, Pa: Herald Press, 1960). My survey of nearly 200 books related to healing and exorcism has led me back once more to the simple service advised by the Apostle James.

29. *The Clergy Manual for Christian Healing* may be ordered from St. Luke's Press, P.O. Box 742, Logansport, IN 46947.

Bibliography

Adams, Jay E. *Competent to Counsel* (Grand Rapids: Baker Book House, 1970).
_____. *The Christian Counselor's Manual* (Grand Rapids: Baker Book House, 1973).
Agel, Jerome. *The Radical Therapist* (New York: Ballantine Books, 1971).
Anderson, Phillip and Phoebe. *The House Church* (New York: Abingdon Press, 1975).
Barclay, William. *Letters to Timothy, Titus, and Philemon* (Philadelphia: Westminster Press, 1960).
Barth, Karl. *Church Dogmatics,* Vol. III (Edinburg: T. and T. Clark, 1958).
Basham, Don. *A Manual for Spiritual Warfare* (Greensburg, Pa.: Manna Books, 1974).
_____. *Can a Christian Have a Demon?* (Monroeville, Pa.: Whitaker Books, 1971).
_____. *Deliver Us from Evil* (Washington Depot, Conn.: Chosen Books, 1972).
_____. *True and False Prophets* (Greensburg, Pa.: Manna Books, 1973).
Bender, Harold. *These Are My People* (Scottdale, Pa.: Herald Press, 1962).
Bender, Ross. *The People of God* (Scottdale, Pa.: Herald Press, 1971).
Benjamin, Alfred. *The Helping Interview* (Boston: Houghton Mifflin, 1969).

Berkhof, Hendrik, trans. by John H. Yoder. *Christ and the Powers* (Scottdale, Pa.: Herald Press, 1962).

Bingham, R. V. *The Bible and the Body* (London: Marshall, Morgan, and Scott, 1939).

Bjornstad, James, and Johnson, Shildes. *Stars, Signs, and Salvation in the Age of Aquarius* (Minneapolis: Bethany Fellowship, 1971).

Blanton, Smiley. *Love or Perish* (New York: Simon and Schuster, 1956).

Blatty, William P. *The Exorcist* (New York: Bantam Books, Inc., 1971, 1974).

Boggs, Wade H. *Faith Healing and the Christian Faith* (Richmond, Va.: John Knox Press, 1956).

Books of Moses or Moses' Magical Spirit Art (Cleveland: The Arthur Westbrook Co.).

Boisen, Anton B. *The Exploration of the Inner World* (Philadelphia: University of Pennsylvania Press, 1971).

Bonnell, J. S. *Do You Want to Be Healed?* (New York: Harper and Row, 1968).

Boom, Corrie Ten. *The Hiding Place* (Old Tappan, N.J.: Chosen Books, 1971).

Brasher, C. W. J. *Faith Healing* (Kemp Hall Press, 1938).

Breeze, Dave. *His Infernal Majesty* (Chicago: Moody Press, 1974).

Bridge, Donald, and Phypers, David. *Spiritual Gifts and the Church* (Downers Grove: Inter-Varsity, 1973).

Bruder, Ernest. *Ministering to Deeply Troubled Persons* (Englewood Cliffs, N.J.: Prentice Hall, 1963).

Carothers, Merlin R. *Prison to Praise* (Plainfield, N.J.: Logos, 1970).

Christenson, James. *Contemporary Worship Service* (Old Tappan, N.J.: Revell, 1971).

Christenson, Larry. *A Charismatic Approach to Social Action* (Minneapolis: Bethany Fellowship, 1974).

——————. *A Message to the Charismatic Movement* (Minneapolis: Dimension Books, 1972).

Clark, Walter H. *Chemical Ecstasy* (New York: Sheed and Ward, Inc., 1969).

Clinebell, Howard J. *Basic Types of Pastoral Counselling* (New York: Abingdon Press, 1966).

Collins, Gary R. *The Christian Psychology of Paul Tournier* (Grand Rapids: Baker, 1973).

_____. *The Fragmented Personality* (Carol Stream, Ill.: Creation House, 1972).

_____. *Overcoming Anxiety* (Wheaton, Ill.: Key, 1973).

Colston, Lowell. *Judgment in Pastoral Counseling* (New York: Abingdon Press, 1966).

Come, Arnold B. *Agents of Reconciliation* (Philadelphia: Westminster Press, 1964).

Complete Edition of the Sixth and Seventh Books of Moses (Cleveland: Arthur Westbrook Co.)

Cooper, John C. *Religion in the Age of Aquarius* (Philadelphia: Westminster Press, 1971).

Cornwall, Judson. *Let Us Praise* (Plainfield, N.J.: Logos, 1973).

Cruz, Nicky. *Satan on the Loose* (Old Tappan, N.J.: Revell, 1973).

Davies, T. W. *Magic, Divination, and Demonology Among the Hebrews and Their Neighbors* (New York: Ktav Publishing Co., 1969).

Davis, John H. *Contemporary Counterfeits* (Winona Lake: BMH Books, 1973).

Dawson, George. *Healing: Pagan and Christian* (London: S.P.C.K., 1935).

De Haan, Richard S. *Satan, Satanism, and Witchcraft* (Grand Rapids: Zondervan, 1972).

Delling, Gerhard. *Worship in the New Testament* (Philadelphia: Westminster Press, 1962).

"Demons," *Catholic Encyclopedia,* Vol. IV (New York: Encyclopedia Press, 1973).

"Demons," *Encyclopedia Judaica,* Vol. V. (New York: Macmillan and Co., 1971).

"Demons," *The Interpreter's Dictionary of the Bible,* Vol. 1 (Nashville: Abingdon Press, 1962).

Dodds, C. H. *The Apostolic Preaching and Its Development*

(New York: Willett Clark and Co., 1937).

Douglas, Mary, ed. *Witchcraft Confessions and Accusations* (New York: Barnes & Noble, 1970).

Drescher, John M. *Spirit Fruit* (Scottdale, Pa.: Herald Press, 1974).

Duncan, A. D. *The Christ, Psychotherapy, and Magic: A Christian Appreciation of Occultism* (London: George Allen and Urwin, Ltd., 1969).

DuPlessis, D. J. *The Spirit Bade Me Go: A Famous Pentecostal Tells His Story* (Plainfield, N.J.: Logos, 1970).

Ebon, Martin. *The Devil's Bride* (New York: Harper & Row, 1975).

Eitren, S. *Some Notes on the Demonology in the New Testament* (Oslave: Typis Expressit, 1950).

Ellis, Albert and Harper, Robert A. *A Guide to Rational Living,* (North Hollywood, Calif.: Wilshire Book Co., 1971).

Ellul, Jacques. *The New Demons* (New York: Seabury, 1975).

Ellwood, Robert S. *Religious and Spiritual Groups in Modern America* (Englewood Cliffs, N.J.: Prentice-Hall, 1973).

Enz, Jacob. *The Christian and Warfare* (Scottdale, Pa.: Herald Press, 1972).

Erdman, Charles R. *Remember Jesus Christ* (Grand Rapids: Eerdmans, 1958).

Ernst, Victor H. *I Talked with Spirits* (Wheaton: Tyndale House, 1970).

Fisher, Walter, *et al. Power, Greed, and Stupidity in the Mental Health Racket* (Philadelphia: Westminster, 1973).

Fitts, William H. *The Experience of Psychotherapy: What It's Like for Client and Therapist* (Princeton, N.J.: D. Van Nostrand Co. 1965).

Ford, Peter S. *The Healing Trinity: Prescription for Body and Mind and Spirit* (New York: Harper & Row, 1971).

Frankl, Victor E. *Man's Search for Meaning* (New York: Washington Square Press, 1968).

_____, trans. by Richard and Clara Winston. *The Doctor and the Soul: An Introduction to Logotherapy* (New York: Alfred A. Knopf, 1955).

Frazier, Claude, ed. *Faith Healing: Finger of God? or Scien-*

tific Curiosity? (New York: Nelson, 1973).

——————. *Should Doctors Play God?* (Nashville: Broadman Press, 1971).

Freed, Stanley and Ruth. *Magic, Witchcraft, and Curing* (New York: Natural History Press, 1967).

Freeman, Hobart E. *Angels of Light* (Plainfield, N.J.: Logos, 1969, 1971).

——————. *Positive Thinking and Confession* (Claypool, Ind.: Faith).

Gasson, Raphael. *The Challenging Counterfeit: A Former Medium Exposes Spiritualism* (Plainfield, N.J.: Logos, 1966, 1972).

Glasser, William. *Reality Therapy* (New York: Harper & Row, 1965).

Glen, Stanley. *The Recovery of the Teaching Ministry* (Philadelphia: Westminster Press, 1960).

Green, Hannah. *I Never Promised You a Rose Garden* (New York: New American Library, 1964).

Gross, Don. *God and Freud* (New York: David McKay, 1959).

——————. *The Case for Spiritual Healing* (New York: Thomas Nelson, 1968).

Haas, Harold I. *The Christian Encounters Mental Illness* (St. Louis: Concordia, 1966).

Haggard, Forrest. *The Clergy and the Craft* (Missouri Lodge of Research: Ovid Bell Press, 1970).

Hagin, Kenneth. *Authority of the Believer* (Tulsa: Kenneth E. Hagin).

Hamilton, Michael, ed. *The Charismatic Movement* (Grand Rapids: Eerdmans, 1975).

Harper, Michael. *Spiritual Warfare: Defeating Satan in the Christian Life* (Plainfield, N.J.: Logos, 1970).

Hauck, Paul. *Reason in Pastoral Counseling* (Philadelphia: Westminster Press, 1972).

——————. *Health and Healing* (Tanzania: Evangelical Lutheran Church, 1967). The Report of the Makumira Consultation on the Healing Ministry of the Church.

Henderson, Glenna. *My Name Is Legion* (Minneapolis:

Bethany Fellowship, 1972).

Hiebert, D. Edmond. *Second Timothy* (Chicago: Moody Press, 1958).

Howe, Ruel L. *The Miracle of Dialogue* (New York: Seabury, 1963).

Ikin, A. Graham. *New Concepts of Healing* (New York: Association Press, 1956).

——————. *Victory Over Suffering* (Great Neck, N.Y.: Channel Press, 1961).

Jacobs, Don. *Demons: An Examination of Demons at Work in the World Today* (Scottdale, Pa.: Herald Press, 1972).

Jahoda, Gustav. *The Psychology of Superstition* (New York: Penguin, 1970).

Jeschke, Marlin. *Discipling the Brother* (Scottdale, Pa.: Herald Press, 1972).

Kallas, James. *Jesus and the Power of Satan* (Philadelphia: Westminster Press, 1968).

——————. *The Real Satan* (Minneapolis: Augsburg,1975).

——————. *The Satanward View: A Study in Pauline Theology* (Philadelphia: Westminster Press, 1966).

Kelly, Henry A. *The Devil, Demonology and Witchcraft; The Development of Christian Beliefs in Evil Spirits* (New York: Doubleday, 1974).

Kelsey, Morton. *Dreams, the Dark Speech of the Spirit* (New York: Doubleday, 1974).

——————. *Encounter with God* (Minneapolis: Bethany Fellowship, 1972).

Kildahl, John P. *The Psychology of Speaking in Tongues* (New York: Harper & Row, 1972).

Klassen, William. *The Forgiving Community* (Philadelphia: Westminster Press, 1966).

Koch, Kurt, E. *Between Christ and Satan* (West Germany: Evangelical Publishers, 1968).

——————. *Christian Counseling and Occultism* (Grand Rapids: Kregel, 1965).

——————. *Day X: The World Situation in the Light of the Second Coming of Christ* (West Germany: Evangelical Publishers, 1967).

_____. *Occult Bondage and Deliverance: Advice for Counseling the Sick, the Troubled, and the Occulty Oppressed* (West Germany: Evangelical Publisher's, 1970).

_____. *The Devil's Alphabet* (West Germany: Evangelical Publishers, 1970).

_____. *The Strife of Tongues* (West Germany: Evangelical Publishers).

_____. *The Revival in Indonesia* (Winona Lake: Spanish World Gospel Broadcasting, Inc., 1970).

Kraus, C. Norman. *The Community of the Spirit* (Grand Rapids: Eerdmans, 1974).

_____. *The Healing Christ* (Scottdale, Pa.: Herald Press, 1972).

Kremer, Emile. *Eyes Opened to Satan's Subtlety: The Origin, Nature, and Consequences of Superstition, Divination, and Magic and the Full Redemption Through the Cross* (Belfast: Raven Publishing Co., 1969).

Langton, Edward. *Satan, A Portrait: A Study of the Character of Satan Through All the Ages* (Folcroft, Pa.: Folcroft, 1973).

Larson, Bruce. *The One and Only You* (Waco: Word Books, 1974).

Leslie, Robert. *Jesus and Logotherapy* (New York: Abingdon Press, 1965).

Lessa, William, and Vogt, Evon A. *A Reading on Comparative Religion* (New York: Harper & Row, 1958, 1972).

Lewis, C. S. *The Screwtape Letters* (New York: Macmillan, 1959).

Lhermitte, Jean, trans. by P. J. Hepburn-Oates. *Diabolical Possession, True and False* (Westminster, Md.: Christian Classics, 1963).

Lind, Millard. *Biblical Foundations for Christian Worship* (Scottdale, Pa.: Herald Press, 1973).

Lindsay, Hal. *Satan Is Alive and Well on Planet Earth* (Grand Rapids: Zondervan, 1973).

Lundström, Gösta, trans. by Joan Bulman. *The Kingdom of God in the Teaching of Jesus* (Richmond, Va.: John Knox, 1963).

MacKintosh, R. H. *The Christian Experience of Forgiveness* (New York: Collins, 1961).

Mairet, Philip, ed. *Christian Essays in Psychiatry* (New York: Philosophical Library, 1956).

Mallory, James D. *The Kink and I* (Grand Rapids: Victor Books, 1974).

Manson, William. *The Way of the Cross* (Richmond, Va.: John Knox, 1958).

Martin, Bernard, trans. by A. A. Jones. *Healing for You* (Richmond, Va.: John Knox, 1963, 1965).

――――――――. *The Healing Ministry of the Church* (London: Lutterworth, 1960).

Maves, Paul, ed. *The Church and Mental Health* (New York: Scribner's 1953).

May, Rollo. *The Art of Counseling* (New York: Abingdon Press, 1967).

McCall, T. S., and Levitt, Zola. *Satan in the Sanctuary* (Chicago: Moody Press, 1973).

McCasland, Vernon. *By the Finger of God* (New York: Macmillan, 1951).

――――――――. *The Pioneer of Our Faith—A New Life of Jesus* (New York: McGraw Hill, 1964).

McGinley, Lawrence J. *Form Criticism of the Synoptic Healing Narratives* (Maryland: Woodstock College Press, 1944).

Mickey, Paul A. *Conflict and Resolution* (New York: Abingdon Press, 1973).

Middleton, John, ed. *Gods and Rituals: Readings in Religious Beliefs and Practices* (Garden City, N.Y.: Natural History Press, 1967).

Middleton, John and Winter, S. H. *Witchcraft and Sorcery in East Africa* (New York: Frederick and Praeger, 1964).

Miller, Paul M. *How God Heals* (Scottdale, Pa.: Herald Press, 1960).

Miller, William A. *Why Do Christians Break Down?* (Minneapolis: Augsburg, 1973).

Montgomery, John W. *Principalities and Powers* (Minneapolis: Bethany Fellowship, 1973).

Moule, C. F. D. *Colossians and Philemon* (New York:

Cambridge University Press, 1968).

Neff, H. Richard. *Psychic Phenomena and Religion: ESP, Prayer Healing, Survival* (Philadelphia: Westminster Press, 1971).

Newbold, H. L. *The Psychiatric Programming of People: Neo-Behavioral Orthomolecular Psychiatry* (New York: Permagon Press, 1972).

Nicola, John J. *Diabolical Possession and Exorcism* (Rockford, Ill.: Tan Books, 1974).

Nouwen, Henri. *The Wounded Healer: Ministry in Contemporary Society* (Garden City, N.Y.: Doubleday, 1972).

Oates, Wayne E. *Anxiety in Christian Experience* (Waco: Word Books, 1971).

_____. *Pastoral Counseling* (Philadelphia: Westminster Press, 1974).

_____. *The Revelation of God in Human Suffering* (Philadelphia: Westminster Press).

_____. *The Psychology of Religion* (Waco: Word Books, 1973).

_____. *When Religion Gets Sick* (Philadelphia: Westminster Press, 1970).

O'Conner, Elizabeth. *Our Many Selves* (New York: Harper & Row, 1971).

Oden, C. Thomas. *The Structure of Awareness* (Nashville: Abingdon Press, 1969).

Oesterreich, T. K. *Possession: Demoniacal and Other* (New York: University Books, 1966).

Offner, Clark, and Straeden, Henry Van. *Modern Japanese Religions* (New York: Twayne, 1963).

Otis, George. *Like a Roaring Lion* (Van Nuys, Calif.: Time-Light Publishing Division of Bible Voice, Inc., 1973).

Oursler, William. *The Healing Power of Faith* (New York: Hawthorne Books, 1957).

Outler, Albert C. *Psychotherapy and the Christian Message* (New York: Harper and Bros., 1954).

Parrinder, Geoffrey. *Worship in the World's Religions* (New York: Association Press, 1959, 1961).

Pelton, Robert W., and Carden, Karen. *Snake Handlers: God*

Fearers? or Fanatics? (New York: Nelson, 1974).

Perls, Fred S. *In and Out of the Garbage Pail* (San Francisco: People Press, 1969).

Peterson, Mary. *Healing, A Spiritual Adventure* (Philadelphia: Fortress, 1974).

Peterson, Robert. *Are Demons for Real?* (Chicago: Moody Press, 1972).

Peterson, William J. *Those Curious New Cults* (New Canaan, Conn.: Keats, 1973).

Petit, Don R., ed. *Exorcism! The Report of a Commission Convened by the Bishop Exeter* (London: S.P.C.K., 1972).

Philpot, Kent. *A Manual of Demonology and the Occult* (Grand Rapids: Zondervan, 1973).

Powell, Jordon. *Release from Guilt and Fear* (New York: Hawthorne Books, 1961).

Pritchard, William H. *Healing by Faith in Christ* (New York: Christian Literature Depot).

Pruyser, Paul W. A. *A Dynamic Psychology of Religion* (New York: Harper & Row, 1968).

Ranaghan, Kevin and Dorothy. *Catholic Pentecostals* (Paramus, N.J.: Paulist Press, 1969).

Reid, Clyde. *Celebrate the Temporary* (New York: Harper & Row, 1972).

Richards, John. *But Deliver Us from Evil* (New York: Seabury Press, 1974).

Richardson, Carl. *Exorcism: New Testament Style* (Old Tappan, N.J.: Revell, 1974).

Riffel, Herman H. *A Living, Loving Way: Christian Maturity and the Spirit's Power* (Minneapolis: Bethany Fellowship, 1973).

Rite of Anointing the Pastoral Care of the Sick (Collegeville, Minn.: The Liturgical Press, 1974).

Roberts, Oral. *The Call: Oral Roberts' Autobiography* (New York: Avon 1971).

Robinson, Wayne A. *I Once Spoke in Tongues* (Wheaton: Tyndale, 1973).

Rose, Louis. *Faith Healing* (New York: Penguin, 1971).

Rose, Stephen C., ed. *Who's Killing the Church?* (Chicago:

City Missionary Society, 1966).

Rouch, Mark. *Competent Ministry* (Nashville: Abingdon Press, 1974).

Sanders, J. Oswald. *Satan Is No Myth* (Chicago: Moody Press, 1975).

Schreiber, Flora R. *Sybil* (Chicago: Henry Regnery, 1973).

Schweizer, Eduard. *Church Order in the New Testament* (London: SCM Press, 1961).

Sharp, Gene. *The Methods of Nonviolent Action* (Boston: Porter Sargent, 1974).

Sherrill, John L. *They Speak with Other Tongues* (Old Tappan, N.J.: Chosen Books, 1965).

Shostrom, Everett. *Man, the Manipulator* (Nashville: Abingdon Press, 1967).

Skrade, Carl. *God and the Grotesque* (Philadelphia: Westminster Press, 1974).

Smith, Nancy C. *Journey Out of Nowhere* (Waco: Word Books, 1973).

Smucker, Leonard. *Spring: A Therapeutic Relationship* (Scottdale, Pa.: Herald Press, 1967).

Southard, Samuel. *Anger in Love* (Philadelphia: Westminster Press, 1973).

Stolz, Karl R. *The Church and Psychotherapy* (New York: Abingdon-Cokesbury Press, 1943).

Stringfellow, William. *An Ethic for Christians and Other Aliens in a Strange Land* (Waco: Word Books, 1973).

Taylor, John V. *The Go-Between God: The Holy Spirit and the Christian Mission* (Philadelphia: Fortress, 1973).

Terhune, William B. *Emotional Problems and What You Can Do About Them* (New York: William Morrow, 1964).

Thielicke, Helmut, trans. by C. C. Barber. *Between God and Satan* (Grand Rapids: Eerdmans, 1959).

Tournier, Paul, and Harnik, Bernard, ed. *Medicine of the Whole Person* (Waco: Word Books, 1973).

Tozer, A. W. *I Talk Back to the Devil* (Harrisburg, Pa.: Christian Publications, 1972).

Unger, Merrill. *Biblical Demonology* (Wheaton: Victor Books, 1952).

_____. *Demons in the World Today* (Wheaton: Tyndale, 1971, 1972).

Vogel, Carl. *Begone Satan* (Collegeville, Minn.: St. John's Abbey, 1935).

Vogt, E. Z., and Lessa, William. *A Reader in Comparative Religion* (New York: Harpers, 1965).

Warnke, Mike. *The Satan Seller* (Plainfield, N.J.: Logos, 1972).

Watkin, Keith. *Liturgies in a Time When Cities Burn* (New York: Abingdon, 1969).

Weatherhead, Leslie D. *Why Do Men Suffer?* (New York: Abingdon).

Weatherspoon, J. B. *Sent Forth to Preach* (New York: Harper and Bros., 1954).

Westberg, Granger. *Nurse, Pastor, and Patient* (Rock Island, Ill.: Augustana Press, 1955).

White, Dale, ed. *Dialogue in Medicine and Theology* (Nashville: Abingdon, 1967).

White, James F. *New Forms of Worship* (New York: Abingdon, 1971).

Whyte, Launcelot. *The Unconscious Before Freud* (New York: Basic Books, 1960).

Wise, Carroll A. *Psychiatry and the Bible* (New York: Harper and Bros., 1942).

_____. *Religion in Illness and Health* (New York: Harper and Bros., 1942).

Wolf, William J. *No Cross, No Crown* (New York: Doubleday, 1957).

Woods, Richard. *The Occult Revolution* (New York: Seabury Press, 1973).

Wright, J. Stafford. *Christianity and the Occult* (Chicago: Moody Press, 1972).

_____. *Man in the Process of Time: A Christian Assessment of the Power and Functions of Human Personality* (Grand Rapids: Eerdmans, 1956).

_____. *Mind, Man, and the Spirits* (Grand Rapids: Zondervan, 1972).

Yoder, John H. *The Politics of Jesus* (Grand Rapids: Eerdmans, 1972).

Yoder, Jonathan G. *Healing: Prayer or Pills?* (Scottdale, Pa.: Herald Press, 1975).

Paul M. Miller, of 1119 South Eighth Street, Goshen, Indiana, is the father of four children and grandfather of four. He is married to the former Bertha S. Mumma. Reared in Lancaster County, Pennsylvania, in the home of a farmer and self-supporting missionary to the Jewish people, he served for some years as a lay-leader in the church.

At 31 years of age, he sold out his dairy farming operation and began training for a pastoral or missionary ministry. During eight years as pastor of the East Goshen Mennonite Church, he earned four degrees, the BA in 1949, the ThB in 1950, the BD in 1952, and the ThM in 1955.

In 1952 he began teaching practical theology at Goshen Biblical Seminary and in 1961 completed work for the ThD at southern Baptist Theological Seminary. His doctoral dissertation was a field study of Christian worship practices and how they compare with creedal affirmations. Over the years he has taught courses in preaching, Christian education, group dynamics, and pastoral counseling.

His experiences in church service include sixteen years as bishop in congregations within the Indiana-Michigan Mennonite Conference, and twenty years as traveling Bible teacher and fraternal worker in eight countries.

From 1966 through 1968 he was researcher for the Association of East African Theological Colleges, helping eleven denominations to rethink their objectives and methods in training African men for the ordained ministry. From 1968 to 1971 he served as Executive Secretary of the Ministerial Committee of the Mennonite Church.

He has functioned as chaplain in three different hospitals and as consultant and facilitator in numerous growth institutes and group dynamics laboratories. He is currently leading marriage counseling and couples communication groups.

He has written numerous articles in journals and three full-length books. *Group Dynamics in Evangelism* (1958), *Servant of God's Servants* (1964), and *Equipping for Ministry in East Africa* (1969).

Asked by Herald Press to rewrite and expand his earlier booklet, *How God Heals,* he branched into a study of exorcism and deliverance ministries. He has lectured on exorcism in more than fifty communities in the United States and Canada.

In 1975 he became accredited as a supervisor of clinical pastoral education and is currently serving in that role in the St. Joe Valley Association for Clinical Pastoral Education, Elkhart, Indiana.